DOES INSPIRATION DEMAND INERRANCY?

Does Inspiration Demand Inerrancy?

A Study of the Biblical Doctrine of Inspiration in the Light of Inerrancy

by
Stewart Custer

THE CRAIG PRESS
Nutley, New Jersey

PHOTOLITHOPRINTED BY CUSHING - MALLOY, INC.
ANN ARBOR, MICHIGAN, UNITED STATES OF AMERICA
1 9 6 8

Dedicated
to my
Wife
who has been
a constant
inspiration

PREFACE

Christian young people often face the question, "Are there errors in the Bible?" The present work is an attempt to survey some of the answers to this question as the Liberals, Neo-Orthodox, Neo-Evangelicals, and strict Conservatives would give them. But the most important answer to this question is the one which Scripture itself gives. As C. J. Vaughan expressed it in his commentary on Hebrews, "The only true view of Inspiration will be that which is the net result of a lifelong study of Scripture itself, with all freedom in registering its phenomena" (p. 312). Similarly, if Scripture does not teach its own inerrancy, why should any Christian be bound to this doctrine? Thus the procedure followed in this work is to present in Part I the teaching of Scripture on the doctrine of Inspiration with special attention to its claims of inerrancy, in Part II to present briefly the different theological opinions on Inspiration, and in Part III to survey some of the passages often advanced as errors to see if there are reasonable explanations.

Special thanks go to Dr. Robert L. Reymond for reading the manuscript and offering many helpful suggestions; to Miss Elizabeth Moore and to Miss Isabel Potts for advice concerning form and style. Any infelicities of thought or expression which remain are the author's sole responsibility.

S. C.

June, 1968

THE AUTHOR

Stewart Custer was born in Chicago, Illinois, in 1931. He holds the following degrees: B.A. *Summa cum laude* in Bible, 1955, M.A. in Bible, 1957, and Ph.D. in Greek text, 1966, Bob Jones University.

In 1955 he began teaching at Bob Jones University as a graduate assistant in Greek, soon became a full professor, and is now chairman of the department of Bible. In the graduate school of Bob Jones University he teaches Biblical Theology, Methods of Bible Exposition, and advanced Greek courses.

Dr. Custer has had a life-long interest in science. In addition to teaching, he is the director of the planetarium at Bob Jones University, producing programs for the public twice a week. He is the author of two booklets, "Problems of Evolution" and "Should a Scientist be an Agnostic?"

He is the editor and originator of the *Biblical Viewpoint,* a theological journal for pastors produced by the graduate faculty of Bob Jones University. To each issue he contributes articles on Biblical theology and exposition; and includes extensive bibliographies of commentaries and other works helpful for the pastor.

Dr. Custer is also in demand as an expository preacher. Not content to teach the theory of preaching, he practices thematic exposition. He is often invited to preach in different churches, sometimes to give a series of expositions on a single book of Scripture. At other times he is asked to speak on special topics such as the Inspiration of Scripture, the fallacies of Evolution, or to deliver an illustrated slide lecture on the Bible and science.

CONTENTS

GLOSSARY

Revelation is the direct communication by God of previously unknown truth.

Illumination is an act of the Holy Spirit enabling any genuine believer to understand the truth.

Inspiration is a supernatural influence of the Holy Spirit on the Biblical writers so that their writings are divinely trustworthy and authoritative.

Verbal Inspiration means that the very words of Scripture are divinely inspired and authoritative.

Plenary Inspiration means full inspiration; every part of Scripture is completely inspired.

Inerrancy is that characteristic of Scripture which renders it without mistake and therefore infallible, not just in religious matters, but also in matters of historic and scientific fact.

Perspicuity refers to that quality of Scripture that enables it to be understood by the average man; Scripture is understandable and clear without the explanations of priests or other religious authorities.

The Dictation Theory is a theory of inspiration which holds that God obliterated the personalities of the Biblical writers and used them as mere machines to record Scripture. Almost all conservatives reject this theory.

The canon is the collection of books which are accepted as the genuine and authoritative rule of faith and practice; to Protestants the canon is synonymous with the 66 books of the Old and New Testaments.

The autographs (or *autographa*) are the original documents written by the prophets and other Biblical writers, copies of which now make up the sources for the books of the Bible.

PART I

THE BIBLICAL TEACHING

Chapter I

THE OLD TESTAMENT TEACHING ON INSPIRATION

Some scholars claim that Scripture does not teach that it is inspired without errors. They therefore charge conservatives with reading into Scripture their own preconceived ideas about inspiration and inerrancy. This charge of adding to Scripture is just as serious as one of taking away from Scripture. Therefore, let us survey the Old Testament in order to see what it teaches concerning its own inspiration. Does Scripture teach a doctrine of inspiration which demands inerrancy, or does it leave room for errors in its message? In many passages in the Old Testament there are clear statements concerning itself and concerning the nature of God's revelation to man. Because the first five books in the Bible are traditionally attributed to Moses, it is appropriate to begin with the description of God's revelation to Moses.

Exodus 4:10-16

God spent eighty years preparing Moses for delivering the Children of Israel from their bondage in Egypt. The preparation was rigorous, but at last the time was fulfilled, and God called Moses to deliver Israel. Moses, however, had had no experience in public speaking for forty years while he had been "at the backside of the desert," and so he began to make excuses for himself.

> And Moses said unto the Lord, O my Lord, I am not eloquent, Neither heretofore, nor since thou hast spoken unto thy servant: but I am slow of speech, and of a slow tongue. And the Lord said unto him, Who hath made man's mouth? or who maketh the dumb, or deaf, or the seeing, or the blind? have not I the Lord? Now therefore go, and I will be with thy mouth, and teach thee what thou shalt say (Ex. 4:10-12).

Notice that the Lord does not say, "I will be with thy mind and teach thee what to think." This is not a communication of thoughts or of concepts alone; this is also a communication of words. "I will be with thy mouth, and teach thee what thou shalt say." This revelation of words is the basis of verbal inspiration.

Even though the Lord promises Moses that He will teach him what to say, Moses is still timid and manufactures excuses. Whenever the Lord gives a commission, He also gives the grace with which to fulfill it. Moses is therefore manifesting a lack of faith by failing to go at once. Scripture adds:

> The anger of the Lord was kindled against Moses, and he said, Is not Aaron the Levite thy brother? I know that he can speak well. . . . And thou shalt speak unto him, and put words in his mouth: and I will be with thy mouth, and with his mouth, and will teach you what ye shall do. And he shall be thy spokesman unto the people: and he shall be, even he shall be to thee instead of a mouth, and thou shalt be to him instead of God (Ex. 4:14-16).

The word *spokesman* in verse 16 is the Hebrew word *Nabhi,* which means *prophet.* The basic meaning of *prophet* is *spokesman,* one who speaks forth the words which another communicates to him. Some scholars will admit that the Word of God was perfect and inerrant when it came to the prophet, but will contend that when the prophet spoke, he spoke in human words which were not inerrant. In this passage, however, the Lord says that Moses shall put words in Aaron's mouth, "and I will be with thy mouth, and with his mouth, and will teach you what ye shall do." In other words God will preserve His revelation from error even in the communications of the prophets themselves.

This does not imply that the prophets were mere machines. God did not obliterate the personalities of the prophets when he communicated His Word to them. Obviously there is a considerable difference in style and vocabulary among the various Biblical writers, but by the inspiration of God their words are divinely trustworthy and authoritative. This is what is meant by verbal inspiration; the words written by the prophets were divinely preserved from error and are therefore God's Words.

EXODUS 31:18; 32:15-16; 34:1

After Moses had been on Mount Sinai for forty days and forty nights, he received a certain revelation from God. The record says that God "gave unto Moses, when he had made an end of communing with him upon Mount Sinai, two tables of testimony, tables of stone, written with the finger of God" (Ex. 31:18). It is plain that the ten commandments were not drawn up by a committee; they were revealed by God alone. The surprising thing about this, however, is the method of communicating them to mankind. Moses was not even allowed to take the ten commandments down by dictation. They were inscribed by the very hand of God; all Moses could do was to receive them from God.

Now some Liberal scholars sneer at Conservatives for believing in a "dictation" theory of inspiration, but consider this passage: these verses imply an inspiration far more sweeping than the "dictation" with which Conservatives are sometimes charged. God inscribed His Words directly on the tablets of stone. The exact words were written by God, and nothing was left to Moses' invention. The Liberals will sometimes inquire, "Why are similar laws found among other ancient peoples?" The answer is that God has put the moral law in the heart of man; and, consequently, human pronouncements of these laws are relatively common, but the ten commandments are a perfect statement of that moral law. In view of the sinful nature of man, God wanted man to have a permanent record of the moral law so that no one could say that God had left man without a witness to his true duty. The ten commandments were therefore communicated with unquestionable authority and trustworthiness.

When God revealed to Moses that the Israelites had sinned in making the golden calf, Scripture says that "Moses turned, and went down from the mount, and the two tables of the testimony were in his hand: the tables were written on both their sides; on the one side and on the other were they written. And the tables were the work of God, and the writing was the writing of God, graven upon the tables" (Ex. 32:15-16). Could there possibly be errors in those ten commandments? If there were errors, whose responsibility was it? If there are errors in this revelation, the responsibility lies with Almighty God. These tables were the handiwork of God Himself. The very words and even the shape of the letters were the responsibility of God. If this does not demand inerrancy, what can? After Moses had broken those tables in his indignation over the sin of the Israelites, the Lord commanded Moses, "Hew thee two tables of stone like unto the first: and I will write upon these tables the words that were in the first tables, which thou brakest" (Ex. 34:1). Obviously, the very words that

God had inspired had to be preserved and communicated to man. Nothing was going to be left to chance or to the memory or imagination of Moses.

NUMBERS 22:28, 38; 23:12, 16, 23-26

Balaam is one of the strangest and most enigmatical of all the personalities in the Old Testament. Although he is a hireling prophet, yet he proclaims the Word of the Lord. Balak, the king of Moab, hires Balaam to curse the Israelites. Because Balak doubts that he can defeat the Israelites militarily, he thus tries to use occult powers to defeat them. Balaam is tempted to go to Balak, but he realizes that he is the spokesman of God. Balak sends many noble princes to Balaam and finally persuades Balaam to come.

On the way to Balak, Balaam rides upon an ass, and as he travels, the ass sees the angel of the Lord standing in the way with a drawn sword in his hand. "And when the ass saw the angel of the Lord, she fell down under Balaam: and Balaam's anger was kindled, and he smote the ass with a staff. And the Lord opened the mouth of the ass, and she said unto Balaam, What have I done unto thee, that thou hast smitten me these three times?" (Num. 22:27-28).

Did the Lord communicate to this ass a general concept and leave it up to the ass to formulate appropriate phraseology? This must mean that the very words were communicated by God. Although it is impossible for an animal to speak, it is not impossible for God to cause an animal to speak. If this is the miraculous activity of the Living God, this passage teaches plainly that God communicated words to this animal and caused it to speak. In the very same way, however, Balaam must speak the Word which God reveals to him, because, when Balaam arrives before king Balak, he says, "Lo, I am come unto thee: *have I now any power at all to say any thing?* the word that God putteth in my mouth, that shall I speak" (Num. 22:38). Thus Balaam puts himself in the same relation to God as the poor ass, which could only speak what God put in its mouth. Balaam had no power to say anything as a prophet except what God granted him. Admittedly, God does not always use this method of inspiring the exact words, but here He did.

Balak does not believe him; the king still thinks that Balaam can say whatever he wants. But when the time comes, Balaam utters blessings upon Israel. When Balak hears this, he cries out, "What hast thou done unto me? I took thee to curse mine enemies, and, behold, thou hast blessed them altogether. And he answered and said, Must I not take heed to speak that which the Lord hath put in my mouth?" (Num. 23:11-12). It was not left up to Balaam as to what phraseology he should use; he was not free to choose what words he wanted. If Balaam was to be a prophet, he had to utter the words which God put in his mouth. It is ridiculous to say that God was this strict in regard to the spoken pronouncements of the prophets, but that when they wrote down in Scripture His Word, He suddenly dismissed all concern as to their phraseology. The same exactness which we see in the spoken revelation is to be expected in the inspiration which guided the prophets when they wrote down God's revelation.

The Scripture is explicit in describing God's dealing with Balaam. It says, "And the Lord met Balaam, and put a word in his mouth, and said, Go again unto Balak, and say thus" (Num. 23:16). There is nothing left to Balaam's discretion; he receives a revelation from God and must proclaim it exactly if he is to be a prophet of the Lord. Thus Balaam continues to bless Israel, saying, "Surely there is no enchantment against Jacob, neither is there any divination against Israel: according to this time it shall be said of Jacob and of Israel, What hath God wrought! Behold, the people shall rise up as a great lion, and lift up himself as a young lion: he shall not lie down until he eat of the prey, and drink the blood of the slain" (Num. 23:23-24). Balak is practically wringing his hands in despair as he cries, "Neither curse them at all, nor bless them at all" (Num. 23:25).

This prophecy was not what Balaam wanted to prophesy; he wanted to prophesy so as to earn all the gifts which Balak had promised him. If Balaam could have twisted his prophecy against Israel, he would have, but it was not within his power to modify the revelation of the Lord and still remain a prophet of the Lord. Because Balaam was faithful in uttering the Word of the Lord, he went on to proclaim one of the great Messianic prophecies, that "there shall come a Star out of Jacob, and a Scepter shall rise out of Israel" (Num. 24:17). It would certainly be strange if the Lord exercised such strict control over this prophet when he uttered these words, and yet exercised no such governing power over the prophet who wrote them down. Clearly the same precision which the Lord enforced in the spoken revelation He also enforced when He inspired the prophet to write down His revelation.

I SAMUEL 10:9-12

After Samuel had anointed Saul king over Israel, he prophesied that Saul would be turned into another person and would prophesy himself. Although Saul was splendid in physical appearance, he was not a very religious person and certainly was not inclined to prophesy, but when he departed from Samuel, "God gave him another heart: and all those signs came to pass that day. And when they came thither to the hill, behold, a company of prophets met him; and the Spirit of God came upon him, and he prophesied among them. And it came to pass, when all that knew him beforetime saw that, behold, he prophesied among the prophets, then the people said one to another, What is this that is come unto the son of Kish? Is Saul also among the prophets?" (I Sam. 10:9-11). Thus Saul had completely changed character by prophesying. This means that when the Spirit of God came upon Saul, he had to utter the prophecies which were given to him. The Spirit turned Saul into something which he was not before. This same kind of control was exercised over all the writing prophets.

II SAMUEL 12:7-9

This is the account in the Old Testament concerning David's sin, that he had Uriah murdered and took Bathsheba as his own wife. After this vile act, David, the backslidden king, sitting on his throne and surrounded by the captains of hundreds and the captains of thousands, is the center of the barbaric splendor of an Oriental court. Nathan the prophet now comes before this Oriental potentate. When the prophet tells the king of a case of injustice done to a poor man, David immediately promises to avenge this wrong. Nathan points his finger at David and thunders forth:

> Thou art the man! Thus saith the Lord God of Israel, I anointed thee king over Israel, and I delivered thee out of the hand of Saul; And I gave thee thy master's house, and thy master's wives into thy bosom, and gave thee the house of Israel and of Judah; and if that had been too little, I would moreover have given unto thee such and such things. Wherefore hast thou despised the commandment of the Lord, to do evil in his sight? thou hast killed Uriah the Hittite with the sword, and hast taken his wife to be thy wife, and hast slain him with the sword of the children of Ammon (II Sam. 12:7-9).

Does this mean that Nathan is just shrewdly guessing at what David had done? Does this mean that Nathan is for the most part correct in what he says about David although there may be errors here and there? Or does it not mean that Nathan comes as God's prophet with an inerrant revelation, knowing that the man on the throne of Israel was a murderer and an adulterer because the Lord God of Israel said so? The answer is self-evident.

II SAMUEL 23:1-2

David was forgiven and fully restored to fellowship with the Lord. At the end of his life his last words are recorded. "David the son of Jesse said, and the man who was raised up on high, the anointed of the God of Jacob, and the sweet psalmist of Israel, said, The Spirit of the Lord spake by me, and his word was in my tongue" (II Sam. 23:1-2). This writer of almost half of the Psalms, the man after God's own heart, disclaims responsibility for his writings and prophecies. Psalm 22 and Psalm 23 were the words of the Spirit of God, not just of David. David was the instrument through whom the Spirit of God spoke. The words were the responsibility of God.

PSALM 2:1

This Psalm is a good example of the inspiration of God working through David. It contains some well-known Messianic prophecies. On one occasion the believers in the early church pray to God, saying, "Lord, thou art God, who hast made heaven, and earth, and the sea, and all that in them is: Who by the mouth of thy servant David hast said" (Acts 4:24-25), and then these believers quote Psalm 2:1-2, "Why do the heathen rage, and the people imagine a vain thing?" Thus the early church agreed with David. This Psalm was not his idea; it was the Word of the Living God spoken through David. God was surely responsible for this Psalm. If there were any errors in it, the fault belonged to God, not just to David. But plainly both in the mind of David and the early church there could be no error in what God had spoken.

PSALM 19:7-11

Again there is a clear testimony to the inerrancy of Scripture. David says, "The law of the Lord is perfect, converting the soul: the testimony of the Lord is sure, making wise the simple" (Ps.

19:7). If the law of God is perfect, are there errors in it? If there is falsehood mingled with the truth, how can this make wise the simple? In the eyes of the psalmist there was no error in the Word of God, nor could there be. His Word was more to be desired than gold.

Psalm 119:9, 89, 97-105

This Psalm deals almost entirely with the Word of God. The psalmist asks, "Wherewithal shall a young man cleanse his way? by taking heed thereto according to thy word" (Ps. 119:9). If there are errors in the Word, could not a young man take heed to it and still not cleanse his way? The psalmist clearly means that the one who takes heed to the Word of God is comparing his life with a perfect standard. He goes on to say, "For ever, O Lord, thy word is settled in heaven" (Ps. 119:89). If there were errors in this Word, why would it be settled in heaven? Does not this presuppose that the Word of God is a divine revelation of the Living God? It is settled in heaven because it is perfect and without errors. The psalmist goes on to say:

> O how love I thy law! it is my meditation all the day. Thou through thy commandments hast made me wiser than mine enemies: for they are ever with me. I have more understanding than all my teachers: for thy testimonies are my meditation. I understand more than the ancients, because I keep thy precepts (Ps. 119:97-100).

This means that the wisest, most venerable counselors of Israel know less than the psalmist, because he knows the written Word of God. Could this be if there were errors in His Word? The wisest men on earth can be mistaken, but in the psalmist's mind the Scriptures cannot be mistaken. If the psalmist were alive today, he would put this into more modern language by saying, "I know more than Karl Barth knows! I know more than Kant or Hegel." Why? Because these men are fallible human beings, they may be mistaken. Even though they may have great intellect, they cannot compare with the infallible Word of God. The psalmist would not say that he understood more than the ancients unless he regarded the Scriptures as perfectly inerrant. Thus the psalmist adds, "Through thy precepts I get understanding: therefore I hate every false way" (Ps. 119:104). The Word of God is true in an absolute sense; all other ways are false. Certainly there could be nothing false in God's Word. "Thy word is a lamp unto my feet, and a light unto my path" (Ps. 119:105). The psalmist just could not conceive of falsehood or error in the Word of God.

ISAIAH 1:10-18

In this prophecy Isaiah is denouncing Israel for its sins. He cries out: "Hear the word of the Lord, ye rulers of Sodom; give ear unto the law of our God, ye people of Gomorrah" (Isa. 1:10). This was not personal animosity against his people, but rather this was the rebuke of Almighty God against the sinfulness of His people. When Isaiah calls them "rulers of Sodom" and "people of Gomorrah," he is not just using bitter invective; he is pronouncing the wrath of God against them. He goes on to say, "To what purpose is the multitude of your sacrifices unto me?" God would not accept sacrifices when there was sin in the life.

Isaiah continues delivering the Word of God by saying, "Wash you, make you clean; put away the evil of your doings from before mine eyes; cease to do evil; learn to do well . . ." (Isa. 1:16 17). Then the prophet utters a great promise: "Come now, and let us reason together, saith the Lord: though your sins be as scarlet, they shall be as white as snow; though they be red like crimson, they shall be as wool" (Isa. 1:18). Was this Isaiah's promise to mankind? No, it was not. Three words in that verse make this clear: "saith the Lord." This is God's promise, not the word of Isaiah alone; therefore, this verse can be a comfort to every one who reads this passage. This is a divine assurance of transformation and forgiveness, not just a human promise. Isaiah is not proclaiming his own word, but the inspired revelation of the Living God.

ISAIAH 30:8-15

God commanded Isaiah to write the words of his prophecy; it was not Isaiah's idea to write a book. The Word of the Lord came to him, saying, "Now go, write it before them in a table, and note it in a book, that it may be for the time to come for ever and ever: That this is a rebellious people, lying children, children that will not hear the law of the Lord" (Isa. 30:8-9). Isaiah did not enjoy saying such words, but this was God's revelation of the sinfulness of His people. Because Isaiah was a prophet of the Lord, he had to communicate this word in all faithfulness. In this whole passage

God, through the prophet, is condemning the sins of Israel. "For thus saith the Lord God, the Holy One of Israel; In returning and rest shall ye be saved; in quietness and in confidence shall be your strength: and ye would not" (Isa. 30:15). Is this the promise of Isaiah? On the contrary this is the promise of "the Lord God, the Holy One of Israel." It would be the wildest presumption for Isaiah to utter such words without the express command of God.

ISAIAH 55:6-11

In this memorable passage which begins, "Ho, every one that thirsteth, come ye to the waters . . ." (Isa. 55:1), the prophet earnestly exhorts Israel to turn to God. He says,

> Seek ye the Lord while he may be found, call ye upon him while he is near: Let the wicked forsake his way, and the unrighteous man his thoughts: and let him return unto the Lord, and he will have mercy upon him; and to our God, for he will abundantly pardon. For my thoughts are not your thoughts, neither are your ways my ways, saith the Lord. For as the heavens are higher than the earth, so are my ways higher than your ways, and my thoughts than your thoughts. For as the rain cometh down, and the snow from heaven, and returneth not thither, but watereth the earth, and maketh it bring forth and bud, that it may give seed to the sower, and bread to the eater: So shall my word be that goeth forth out of my mouth: it shall not return unto me void, but it shall accomplish that which I please, and it shall prosper in the thing whereto I sent it (Isa. 55:6-11).

This does not refer to the word of Isaiah, but to the Word of God. This divine Word cannot fail to accomplish the purpose for which God gives it. God sends His Word with omnipotent power to fulfill His purpose. If this must be limited to the word of Isaiah, the thought is foolish. This great offer of forgiveness, however, is obviously the Word of God. Although God's thoughts may transcend the thoughts of man, yet God sends His Word with inerrant precision to man in order that it may fulfill His purpose.

JEREMIAH 1:4-9

The prophet Jeremiah describes his call and commission by saying,

> Then the word of the Lord came unto me, saying, Before I formed thee in the belly I knew thee; and before thou camest forth out of the womb I sanctified thee, and I ordained thee a prophet

unto the nations. Then said I, Ah, Lord God! behold, I cannot speak: for I am a child. But the Lord said unto me, Say not, I am a child: for thou shalt go to all that I shall send thee, and whatsoever I command thee thou shalt speak. Be not afraid of their faces: for I am with thee to deliver thee, saith the Lord. Then the Lord put forth his hand, and touched my mouth. And the Lord said unto me, Behold, I have put my words in thy mouth (Jer. 1:4-9).

Jeremiah did not want to receive such a call, because he knew that he was sent to a wicked and rebellious people who were soon going into captivity. But God called him anyway and put the divine Words into his mouth. It was not left up to Jeremiah's discretion as to what he would say and what he would omit. He had to deliver the Word of God as it was communicated to him. Notice that God put His Words in Jeremiah's mouth; it was not thoughts, but words that God communicated to him. This can only mean that when he wrote, it was with verbal inspiration, but beyond this, God is responsible for any errors in the message, for Jeremiah is to proclaim only what God communicated to him.

JEREMIAH 23:16-22, 28-31, 36

There were many false prophets in Israel and Judah throughout their histories. The outstanding mark of the true prophet of the Lord was his faithfulness in proclaiming exactly what the Lord had revealed to him. On a number of occasions the true prophets had to resist the false. Therefore the Lord spoke to Jeremiah, saying, "Hearken not unto the words of the prophets that prophesy unto you: they make you vain: they speak a vision of their own heart, and not out of the mouth of the Lord" (Jer. 23:16). Thus the prophet who speaks from his own heart is not the prophet of the Lord, for the true prophets speak only what the Lord commands.

The false prophets had been promising peace and prosperity. Although the sins of the Israelites had been increasing, these false prophets had said, "No evil shall come upon you" (Jer. 23:17). In reality the fury of the Lord had gone forth against the sinfulness of His people; therefore, the Lord rebuked them by saying, "I have not sent these prophets, yet they ran: I have not spoken to them, yet they prophesied" (Jer. 23:21). If these prophets had been faithful in proclaiming the message of the Lord, the people would have turned from their evil ways, but these prophets had not denounced the sins of the Israelites.

When the Lord addressed the prophets themselves, He commanded them to speak His Word with all fidelity. "The prophet that hath a dream, let him tell a dream; and he that hath my word, let him speak my word faithfully" (Jer. 23:28). This was the secret of the power which the true prophets wielded; the Word they uttered was the Word of God. When the Lord refers to His Word, He speaks always as though it was an invincible power. "Is not my word like as a fire? saith the Lord; and like a hammer that breaketh the rock in pieces?" (Jer. 23:29). Although the sinner's heart may be as hard as a rock, the Word of God can break that hard heart and can purge away the dross in the life more surely than any fire.

Only the true Word of the Lord can accomplish this; therefore, the Lord spoke to Jeremiah to condemn the false prophets: "Behold, I am against the prophets, saith the Lord, that use their tongues, and say, He saith" (Jer. 23:31). Yet this is the very thing that Liberals think the prophets did: they think that the prophets used the formula "Thus saith the Lord" as a mere rhetorical device to emphasize their uninspired preaching. But God spoke in bitter condemnation against the prophets who did this. The punishment of God hung suspended over every prophet who tried to change the Word of the Lord; hence the Lord commanded them: "And the burden of the Lord shall ye mention no more: for every man's word shall be his burden; for ye have perverted the words of the living God, of the Lord of hosts our God" (Jer. 23:36). The true prophet of God did not dare utter a message which the Lord had not given him.

JEREMIAH 26:2, 8

In this passage the Word of the Lord came to Jeremiah again, saying, "Thus saith the Lord; Stand in the court of the Lord's house, and speak unto all the cities of Judah, which come to worship in the Lord's house, all the words that I command thee to speak unto them; diminish not a word" (Jer. 26:2). Not even one word could Jeremiah omit; he had to proclaim every word which the Lord communicated to him. No matter how unpleasant the message, Jeremiah could not diminish even one word.

Because Jeremiah was faithful in fulfilling this commission, "the priests and the prophets and all the people took him, saying, Thou shalt surely die" (Jer. 26:8). Even though he was threatened with death, Jeremiah would not omit a single word from his message because the message he delivered was the Word of the Living God.

JEREMIAH 36:4-8, 14-19, 20-25, 27-30

The Lord commanded Jeremiah to take the roll of a book and to write in it all the words which the Lord had spoken against sinful Israel and Judah. When Jeremiah summoned a scribe, Baruch, the Bible says that "Baruch wrote from the mouth of Jeremiah all the words of the Lord, which he had spoken unto him, upon a roll of a book" (Jer. 36:4). Since Jeremiah was not free, he commanded Baruch to take the roll and to read it to the people in the house of the Lord, in the hope that they would turn from their evil way and obey the Word of the Lord. After Baruch had read this scroll to the people, the rulers and nobles of Israel sent for Baruch and commanded him to bring the scroll.

> And they said unto him, Sit down now, and read it in our ears. So Baruch read it in their ears. Now it came to pass, when they had heard all the words, they were afraid both one and other, and said unto Baruch, We will surely tell the king of all these words. And they asked Baruch, saying, Tell us now, How didst thou write all these words at his mouth? Then Baruch answered them, He pronounced all these words unto me with his mouth, and I wrote them with ink in the book. Then said the princes unto Baruch, Go, hide thee, thou and Jeremiah; and let no man know where ye be (Jer. 36:15-19).

They knew what these words would mean; a stirring denunciation of a wicked king would surely bring persecution, but they took the scroll and told the king about it. Then the king commanded one of the princes to read the scroll.

> And Jehudi read it in the ears of the king, and in the ears of all the princes which stood beside the king. Now the king sat in the winterhouse in the ninth month: and there was a fire on the hearth burning before him. And it came to pass, that when Jehudi had read three or four leaves, he cut it with the penknife, and cast it into the fire that was on the hearth, until all the roll was consumed in the fire that was on the hearth. Yet they were not afraid, nor rent their garments, neither the king, nor any of his servants that heard all these words (Jer. 36:21-24).

It never occurred to any of these men to be afraid to touch the Word of the Living God. But the Word which God intends men to hear and to read cannot be so easily destroyed.

> Then the word of the Lord came to Jeremiah . . . saying, Take thee again another roll, and write in it all the former words that were in the first roll, which Jehoiakim the king of Judah hath burned. And thou shalt say to Jehoiakim king of Judah, Thus saith the Lord; Thou hast burned this roll, saying, Why hast thou written therein, saying, The king of Babylon shall certainly come and destroy this land. . . . Therefore thus saith the Lord of Jehoiakim king of Judah; He shall have none to sit upon the throne of David: and his dead body shall be cast out in the day to the heat, and in the night to the frost (Jer. 36:27-30).

This king who rose up and dared to burn the scroll which contained the Word of the Living God shall be cut off in judgment. The body of the king shall lie exposed to the heat by day and the frost by night. This Word of God cannot be destroyed. Woe to the man who tries! Thus the scroll had to be written again, and every one of the former words had to be preserved. It was not just the thoughts that counted, but the words. The Words that Jeremiah had written were preserved and are with us today; Jehoiakim was indeed slain in judgment. It is not possible for the Word of God to be mistaken — or destroyed. No wonder that the prophets proclaimed it boldly and fearlessly. All power in heaven and earth stood behind that Word.

EZEKIEL 3:4-11

When God commissioned the prophet Ezekiel, He commanded him, "Son of man, go, get thee unto the house of Israel, and speak with my words unto them" (Ezek. 3:4). Ezekiel was not to use his own words, but rather the words which God revealed to him. Although Ezekiel was faithful in delivering the message of the Lord, the sinful people would not listen to his message, but the Lord charged Ezekiel not to be afraid of them. The prophet went on to say, "Moreover he said unto me, Son of man, all my words that I shall speak unto thee receive in thine heart, and hear with thine ears. And go, get thee to them of the captivity, unto the children of thy people, and speak unto them, and tell them, Thus saith the Lord God; whether they will hear, or whether they will forbear" (Ezek. 3:10-11).

All the words which God communicated to him Ezekiel had to speak; the prophet was not free to change the message. He was to declare the Word of God whatever the response of the Israelites. Certainly the words which Ezekiel wrote down by the inspiration of God were just as surely communicated to him by God. Whether the revelation from God was spoken or written, Ezekiel declared it or wrote it with the confidence that God was responsible for the message; he felt that he himself was only the spokesman.

DANIEL 2:19-23, 26-28

Nebuchadnezzar, king of Babylon, had a dream of the great image. But when none of the wise men of Babylon could tell him the dream, he commanded that they all should be slain. Such a decree would include Daniel as well. When Daniel heard of the decree, he and his friends prayed to God to reveal the king's dream to them.

> Then was the secret revealed unto Daniel in a night vision. Then Daniel blessed the God of heaven. Daniel answered and said, Blessed be the name of God for ever and ever: for wisdom and might are his. And he changeth the times and the seasons: he removeth kings, and setteth up kings: he giveth wisdom unto the wise, and knowledge to them that know understanding: He revealeth the deep and secret things: he knowth what is in the darkness, and the light dwelleth with him. I thank thee, and praise thee, O thou God of my fathers, who hast given me wisdom and might, and hast made known unto me now what we desired of thee: for thou hast now made known unto us the king's matter (Dan. 2: 19-23).

This secret dream was entirely beyond the capabilities of man to perceive; consequently, it could be made known only by God. In his prayer Daniel made clear that God is the source of wisdom and the revealer of secret things. When Daniel claimed to know the dream, they brought him in before the king in haste. King Nebuchadnezzar inquired of Daniel, "Art thou able to make known unto me the dream which I have seen, and the interpretation thereof?" Daniel replied boldly:

> The secret which the king hath demanded cannot the wise men, the astrologers, the magicians, the soothsayers, shew unto the king; But there is a God in heaven that revealeth secrets, and maketh known to the king Nebuchadnezzar what shall be in the latter days. Thy dream, and the visions of thy head upon thy bed, are these . . . (Dan. 2:27-28).

No human being could tell the king this secret, but there is a God in heaven that can reveal exact truth to man. Daniel spoke with the boldness of a man who could not possibly be wrong. It never occurred to Daniel that there could be the slightest error in any of the details which he was making known to the king. The God who can set up kings and remove them will certainly be able to communicate a revelation to His prophet without making an error. In Daniel's mind the Word that God communicated to him was absolutely infallible.

Amos 3:1, 7-8; 7:12-16

The prophet Amos was sent to prophesy to a rebellious and sinful people. Although he did not want to denounce them, he had to be faithful in proclaiming the revelation which God gave to him. He cried out: "Hear this word that the Lord hath spoken against you, O children of Israel" (Amos 3:1). He was not speaking his personal opinion; he was declaring the Word that God had uttered against them. He continued by saying: "Surely the Lord God will do nothing, but he revealeth his secret unto his servants the prophets. The lion hath roared, who will not fear? the Lord God hath spoken, who can but prophesy?" (Amos 3:7-8).

When a lion roars, the people who are nearby do not calmly reflect on whether they shall be afraid or not; they are simply terrified. In the same way when the Lord God has spoken, the prophet cannot decide what he shall speak and what he shall leave out; he must proclaim all that God has revealed, even when this means persecution and sorrow. Amos was most faithful to God in denouncing the sins of Israel, but he had to face bitter retaliation, as he said:

> Amaziah said unto Amos, O thou seer, go, flee thee away into the land of Judah, and there eat bread, and prophesy there: But prophesy not again any more at Bethel: for it is the king's chapel, and it is the king's court. Then answered Amos, and said to Amaziah, I was no prophet, neither was I a prophet's son; but I was an herdman, and a gatherer of sycomore fruit: And the Lord took me as I followed the flock, and the Lord said unto me, Go, prophesy unto my people Israel. Now therefore hear thou the word of the Lord . . . (Amos 7:12-16).

When Amos was threatened, he reminded his adversary that he did not choose to become a prophet, but God had called him and had commanded him to prophesy against Israel. Therefore he was uttering fiery denunciations of the sins of Israel, not because he wanted to, but because it was the Word of the Living God, and he could not change it. This was the characteristic attitude of all the prophets.

MICAH 3:8-12

Micah also had to denounce the sins of Israel and Judah. Although this was a painful task, he, too, uttered the Word of the Lord faithfully. But he disclaimed any responsibility for his prophecies; God had called him to the task and had empowered him for it. He said that "truly I am full of power by the spirit of the Lord, and of judgment, and of might, to declare unto Jacob his transgression, and to Israel his sin" (Mic. 3:8). It was the Spirit of God who moved Micah to cry out against the sins of his people. Hear his impassioned cry:

> They build up Zion with blood, and Jerusalem with iniquity. The heads thereof judge for reward, and the priests thereof teach for hire, and the prophets thereof divine for money. . . . Therefore shall Zion for your sake be plowed as a field, and Jerusalem shall become heaps . . . (Mic. 3:10-12).

This was not what Micah wanted to say, but this was the judgment that Almighty God pronounced against His sinful people. Micah was only the spokesman. It never occurred to any of these prophets that their prophecies might be mistaken. God was the One who had commanded them to speak; God was the One who was responsible for the truth of their prophecies. If there are errors in Scripture, God must be charged with making the mistakes. To the prophet this was simply unthinkable.

Although the prophets were keenly aware of human frailty, their experience of the power of God resting upon them gave them a serene assurance that their prophecies would be fulfilled. The inspiration which impelled them to write also rendered their writings infallible. It was not that they could not err; it was rather that the God of truth would not let them err. Never do we hear a prophet of the Lord say: "I think that this is right." Can you imagine Amos saying, "I hope that this is the Word of the Lord"?

The personalities of the prophets certainly do color their writings, but the inspiration of God rendered their writings the

Word of the Living God. God claims to be able to fashion the mouth of man and to be able to control its utterances. The prophets delivered their messages in the supreme confidence that He was actually speaking through them. We are not reading into Scripture the theory of an inerrant inspiration; this is the faith of the prophets themselves. Anyone who reads these passages with an open mind ought to be able to see that the prophets directly taught that their messages were the inerrant Word of the God who is truth and who cannot lie or mislead. They never uttered the phrase *Thus saith the Lord* in hypocrisy.

CHAPTER II

THE NEW TESTAMENT TEACHING ON INSPIRATION

The New Testament is the heart of the Scriptural teaching about inspiration. In the New Testament our Lord Jesus Christ comments on the value and authority of the Old Testament Scriptures; the apostles compare their own writings with the Old Testament. This is definitive for the Scriptural doctrine of inspiration.

The Old Testament prophets disowned all responsibility for the words which they uttered under the inspiration of God; they were not proclaiming their own words or opinions, but rather the Words of the Living God. The prophets spoke forth in all faithfulness the words which God commanded them to speak, and the responsibility for the fulfillment of these prophecies rested on God alone. The prophet was not an originator but a spokesman for God. The New Testament continues this same teaching that all responsibility for the truth of Scripture rests on God, not the human spokesman.

MATTHEW 1:22

When the angel of the Lord came to Joseph to describe the birth of the Lord Jesus Christ, he told Joseph that Mary would bring forth a child, and that Joseph should call His name "Jesus: for he shall save his people from their sins." Matthew commented on this by saying, "Now all this was done, that it might be fulfilled which was spoken by the Lord through the prophet, saying, Behold, a virgin shall be with child, and shall bring forth a son, and they shall call his name Emmanuel, which being interpreted is, God with us" (Matt. 1:22-23).[1] The terminology which Matthew used shows that he is in complete agreement with what the prophets of the Old Testament had said concerning the inspiration of God. Isaiah 7:14 had been spoken, according to Matthew, "by the Lord through the prophet."[1] This means that the responsibility for the fulfillment of that prophecy did not rest with Isaiah, but with God Himself. The message of Isaiah was the message of God; Isaiah was His spokesman. Since this is what Isaiah himself taught about his prophecies, Matthew is in thorough agreement with the Old Testament doctrine of inspiration.

MATTHEW 2:4-6

In the days of Herod, the king of the Jews, the wise men came from the east to inquire where the new born King of the Jews could be found. Herod acted swiftly, "and when he had gathered all the chief priests and scribes of the people together, he demanded of them where Christ should be born" (Matt. 2:4). In any such gathering of religious authorities would not some disagreement be likely? Would not some suggest one place and some another? Would not others say that no one could tell? On the contrary there was a single, unanimous answer given without hesitation or question. "And they said unto him, In Bethlehem of Judaea: for thus it is written by the prophet, And thou Bethlehem, in the land of Juda, art not the least among the princes of Juda: for out of thee shall come a Governor, that shall rule my people Israel" (Matt. 2:6). The matter was settled. There was no need for further inquiry or discussion; the prophet had spoken! Clearly in their thinking God had revealed His will through the prophet.

Does this mean that there could be a mistake in this prophecy? Is it possible that the prophet could be in error about where the Messiah was to be born? On the contrary, the prophet has given forth the true and infallible Word of God; therefore Bethlehem must be the place from which the Messiah is to come. The selection of Bethlehem was not left to the prophet's discretion; he was merely the spokesman of what God had determined. This account portrays the attitude of the average Jew in the first century world. He regarded the messages of the prophets as the Word of God. Plainly he did not think that there was any possibility of a mistake in what the prophets proclaimed as the Word of God.

MATTHEW 4:4, 7, 10

This passage presents the sharpest contrast in the New Testament between Christ and Satan, truth and error, light and darkness,

the Saviour of the world and the seducer of the world. This is
the temptation of our Lord. After the Lord has fasted for forty
days and forty nights, the devil comes to Him and says, "If thou
be the Son of God, command that these stones be made bread"
(Matt. 4:3). This was certainly a logical temptation after such a
long period of abstaining from food. The Lord Jesus Christ could
have drawn upon His innate power as the Son of God and could
have struck Satan to the ground with a thunderbolt of His divinity,
but He did not. He chose instead to use the sword of the Spirit,
the Word of God, which is the same weapon that is available for
every believer.

The Lord answers Satan, "It is written, Man shall not live by
bread alone, but by every word that proceedeth out of the mouth
of God" (Matt. 4:4). He quotes from the Scriptures to defeat
Satan. Notice that there is no rebuttal. Satan does not say, "You're
only quoting from Deuteronomy; there may be an error there!"
Satan drops the subject completely because falsehood has been
revealed by the truth. Although Satan has no comment to make
on this set-back, he is very resourceful and tries again.

This time Satan quotes Scripture himself; the devil can quote
Scripture, too, when it suits his purposes. Now Satan takes Christ
up to the pinnacle of the temple and in effect says, "You want
to be received as the Messiah; therefore cast yourself off before
this multitude, and they will accept you. You can't hurt yourself,
for it is written, 'He shall give his angels charge concerning thee:
and in their hands they shall bear thee up, lest at any time thou
dash thy foot against a stone'" (Matt. 4:6). But again Christ
answers with a stroke from the sword of the Spirit, "It is written
again, Thou shalt not tempt the Lord thy God" (Matt. 4:7).
Satan has no answer to this either. The Word of God is the truth
and has revealed Satan's dishonest use of Scripture to persuade
Christ to act apart from the will of God. The misinterpretation
of Scripture has no effect on Christ, whose Word it is.

Satan tries one last time to defeat the Lord. He takes the
Lord up to a high mountain and shows Him all the kingdoms of
the world and says, "All these things will I give thee, if thou
wilt fall down and worship me" (Matt. 4:9). For the third time
Christ uses a stroke from the sword of the Spirit to defeat Satan.
"It is written, Thou shalt worship the Lord thy God, and him only
shalt thou serve" (Matt. 4:10). Christ takes no advantage over
us in this contest. He uses the same weapon which we have,

the Sword of the Spirit, and with stroke after stroke after stroke He wins complete victory; Satan goes down in utter defeat. "Then the devil leaveth him" (Matt. 4:11). The sword of the Spirit is absolute truth; error cannot stand in its presence. Satan has no answer to the truth. Falsehood stands revealed by the Word of the Living God.

MATTHEW 5:18

The Lord Jesus Christ refers to the Old Testament Scriptures by saying, "Think not that I am come to destroy the law, or the prophets: I am not come to destroy, but to fulfill. For verily I say unto you, Till heaven and earth pass, one jot or one tittle shall in no wise pass from the law, till all be fulfilled" (Matt. 5:17-18). The *jot* is the Hebrew *yodh*, the smallest letter of the Hebrew alphabet, which looks like an apostrophe in English. The *tittle* is a small horn or projection on a Hebrew letter that changes it from one letter to another. This is similar to the way a small line changes an *O* to a *Q* in English.

Therefore our Lord is teaching that the smallest letter and even the smallest distinguishing part of a letter must be fulfilled if it is in the Old Testament Scripture. But if there are errors in the Old Testament, why would it have to be fulfilled? Why would not Christ say "That part of Scripture which is true must be fulfilled"? Why does Christ say that the smallest letter and the smallest part of a letter must be fulfilled? The reason is that the Old Testament is the infallible, inerrant Word of the Living God. Errors cannot exist in it.

MATTHEW 15:1-9

When the scribes and the Pharisees come to Jesus, they ask Him a leading question, "Why do thy disciples transgress the tradition of the elders? for they wash not their hands when they eat bread" (Matt. 15:2). Although these leaders think that they can trap Him by their ceremonial traditions, He has the answer for them. He asks, "Why do ye also transgress the commandment of God by your tradition?" (Matt. 15:3). By this He shows that the Scriptures are not the traditions of men. The Scriptures are contrasted with such tradition. The ceremonial regulations with which the Pharisees wished to burden men were the traditions of men; in contrast to these, the Scriptures were the commandment of God. The Scriptures are not the opinions of men, but rather the necessary and authoritative revelation of God to man. Men's traditions may be dispensed with; the Scriptures may not be.

The Lord goes on to say to these scribes and Pharisees, "Ye hypocrites, well did Esaias prophesy of you, saying, This people draweth nigh unto me with their mouth, and honoureth me with their lips; but their heart is far from me. But in vain they do worship me, teaching for doctrines the commandments of men" (Matt. 15:7-9). If they will receive it, Christ is willing to teach them the Scriptures, the commandments of God, but these petty Pharisees wish to teach the commandments of men instead. A sharper contrast could not be made: the Scriptures are the commandments of God; the traditions of men are not.

MATTHEW 22:29-32, 42-45

On another occasion several groups of the enemies of the Lord come to Him to try to snare Him in His talk. After the Lord has answered the question of the Pharisees with His usual wisdom, the Sadducees come to pose a hypothetical problem for Him. Since the Sadducees did not believe in a resurrection, they decide to use this doctrine to ensnare Him. They told Him that a certain woman was married to a man who died, and according to Jewish tradition, his eldest brother married the woman to raise up children for his brother, so that his brother's name would not die out in Israel. There were seven brothers. Each of them married this woman, and each in his turn died. Finally the woman also died. Now they pose their insolvable problem: "Therefore in the resurrection whose wife shall she be of the seven? for they all had her" (Matt. 22:28). One can almost see the triumphal smirk on their faces as they pose their trap.

But Jesus has a powerful answer for them. He says, "Ye do err, not knowing the scriptures, nor the power of God" (Matt. 28:29). Does this mean that there can be error in Scripture? On the contrary, the reason these Sadducees erred was that they did not know the Scriptures. The Scriptures are the truth; the man who knows and obeys the sacred Scriptures does not err because he is obeying a standard of infallible truth. The Sadducees err because they do not know the Scriptures. Jesus adds a significant point here. They err not only because they do not know the Scriptures, but also because they do not know the power of God either. It is not enough to have a cold, dead, intellectual fund of information. That is not the kind of knowledge to which Christ refers. He means that knowledge which is an experience of the power of God in the heart and life. If a man has experienced this power in his heart, then this knowledge has been translated into life. The believer must know the Scriptures and must know in his heart the power of God as well. Both knowledge and experience are necessary.

In this instance, the knowledge of which the Sadducees were ignorant was the resurrection; consequently, the Lord draws a fine interpretation from the Old Testament statement of God, "I am the God of Abraham, and the God of Isaac, and the God of Jacob" (Matt. 22:32). Even the unbelieving Sadducees would not be blasphemous enough to say that God was the God of the dead. Therefore Abraham, Isaac, and Jacob had to live, for "God is not the God of the dead, but of the living." Thus the Lord stresses the exact words in order to bring forth an important doctrine from an Old Testament passage.

When they are all through asking Him question, He turns the tables on them and asks them a question. "What think ye of Christ? whose son is he? They say unto him, The son of David. He saith unto them, How then doth David in spirit call him Lord, saying, The Lord said unto my Lord, Sit thou on my right hand, till I make thine enemies thy footstool?" (Matt. 22:42-44). Although it is usual for the descendant to use terms of reverence in speaking of an ancestor, in this instance it was appropriate for David to call his descendant *Lord* because his descendant was the Messiah, the divine Son of God. Again the Lord has drawn a great doctrine out of an Old Testament passage by a very discriminating interpretation of the exact words of Scripture. This remains an example for all believers. The words of Scripture are authoritative and inerrant.

LUKE 16:29-31

In the account of the rich man and Lazarus, Christ described how the rich man died and went to his torment in Hades. There the rich man complains that his brothers ought to have a better chance than he had and asks Abraham to send Lazarus to them. Abraham replies, "They have Moses and the prophets: let them hear them" (Luke 16:29). The rich man implies that the written

Word was inadequate; Abraham declares that the Scriptures are completely adequate and adds, "If they hear not Moses and the prophets, neither will they be persuaded, though one rose from the dead" (Luke 16:31). At the very least, this is an impressive estimate of the Old Testament Scriptures; at the most, this implies that the sacred Scriptures are an infallible revelation of the will of God.

LUKE 24:25-27, 44-45

After the resurrection of the Lord, two disciples were going to the village of Emmaus. The Lord Jesus Christ manifested Himself to them and talked with them concerning the events of the crucifixion and the resurrection. When the disciples expressed an attitude of despondency, the Lord said to them, "O fools, and slow of heart to believe all that the prophets have spoken: Ought not Christ to have suffered these things, and to enter into his glory?" (Luke 24:25-26). The object of faith ought to be "all that the prophets have spoken." If there were errors mixed in with the truth, why would the Lord thus give unqualified approval to the entire Old Testament? Not content with this, the Lord then took the Scriptures and explained their true meaning concerning Himself. "And beginning at Moses and all the prophets, he expounded unto them in all the scriptures the things concerning himself" (Luke 24:27). Plainly, there was not a single error in Scripture which He had to correct.

Later when He appeared to the disciples in the upper room, He again took up this subject and said, "These are the words which I spake unto you, while I was yet with you, that all things must be fulfilled, which were written in the law of Moses, and in the prophets, and in the psalms, concerning me. Then opened he their understanding, that they might understand the scriptures" (Luke 24:44-45). This threefold division of the Old Testament into the law, the prophets, and the psalms (or the writings) was the usual Jewish way of describing the entire Old Testament Scriptures. It was all equally authoritative and infallible in its statements. Although the Jews honored Moses above all, they would not think of saying that there were more errors in the writings of Isaiah than in the writings of Moses. To them, the Scriptures were the voice of God. When there is a difficult passage the fault is always with man's understanding or comprehension, not with the Scriptures themselves.

JOHN 5:38-40, 45-47

Jesus again confronts His adversaries and reproaches them for not receiving the testimony of John the Baptist concerning Himself. He reminds them that God the Father had also testified of Him at the baptism, and He adds, "Ye have not his word abiding in you: for whom he hath sent, him ye believe not. Search the scriptures; for in them ye think ye have eternal life: and they are they which testify of me. And ye will not come to me, that ye might have life" (John 5:38-40). The Lord charges His adversaries with repudiating the Word which God had communicated to them, and therefore He also charges them to "search the Scriptures," to examine with care and diligence these holy Writings.[2] They thought that they had eternal life in them, but they would not come to Christ, and thus they did not have life. The Lord Jesus Christ is the great Subject of Scripture; these Jews who refused Him could not understand Scripture. The person who has not given his allegiance to Christ cannot truly understand or appreciate the Scriptures.

Christ addresses His adversaries again, saying, "Do not think that I will accuse you to the Father: there is one that accuseth you, even Moses, in whom ye trust. For had ye believed Moses, ye would have believed me: for he wrote of me" (John 5:45-46). This shows that the Liberals who claim to receive the sayings of Jesus while they repudiate the "barbaric" Old Testament with all its bloody sacrifices do not receive the true Lord Jesus Christ. The Lord gives His estimate of the Old Testament: it was a testimony concerning Himself. Moses himself had prophesied of the coming of the Lord. The man who truly believes the writings of Moses finds himself led to believe in the Lord Jesus Christ. The man who rejects the Old Testament will not believe completely in the New Testament either.

JOHN 6:63

On another occasion after the Lord Jesus has been teaching in the synagogue in Capernaum, He says to His disciples, "It is the spirit that quickeneth; the flesh profiteth nothing: the words that I speak unto you, they are spirit, and they are life" (John 6:63). It is not just the thoughts or concepts that the Lord is proclaiming that will transform the lives of men. The very words which He utters are spirit and are life. The Greek word in this passage for "word," *rhema,* is the one for a grammatical word rather than an idea or thought. The words of the Lord Jesus had the power of God resting upon them. This is further evidence for the doctrine of verbal inspiration.

JOHN 7:16-17

When the Lord Jesus teaches in the temple, the Jews marvel at His doctrine, but He answer them, "My doctrine is not mine, but his that sent me. If any man will do his will, he shall know of the doctrine, whether it be of God, or whether I speak of myself" (John 7:16-17). The Lord Jesus Christ was not a mere human thinker; He was the divine Son of God, and the words which He spoke carried divine authority. The man who is willing to obey God can know whether Christ's teaching is human or divine, but the person who will not obey need not expect any illumination on the content of Christ's message. It would be incredible if the doctrine which Christ obviously thought was the doctrine of God should be really filled with errors.

JOHN 8:26, 28, 31-32, 40, 47

On a different occasion when the Lord Jesus was teaching the people, He mentions God the Father and says, "He that sent me is true; and I speak to the world those things which I have heard of him" (John 8:26). It is not the character of God to mingle error with the truth. God the Father is true, and the Lord Jesus was faithful in proclaiming to the world those things which the Father had communicated to Him. Again and again the Lord Jesus attributes all the authority for His words to the Father: "I do nothing of myself; but as my Father hath taught me, I speak these things" (John 8:28).

When many of the Jews believe on Him, He says to them, "If ye continue in my word, then are ye my disciples indeed; And ye shall know the truth, and the truth shall make you free" (John 8:31-32). Today many people will say that the test of the Christian is love, not doctrine. They stress that if we love one another, men will know that we are His disciples. Love is not enough; it is necessary to continue in the Word of Christ as well. The person who rejects the revealed Word of God cannot make up for it by trying to love everyone. In no place does the Word of God exalt love above the truth. If love is important for the believer, so is the truth! The mark of the true believer is to continue in the Word of Christ.

The believer who does continue in Christ's Word can expect to know the truth and to be made free by it. This is contrary to those who say that man can never come to a real knowledge of divine truth; Christ here promises that a man can. But what if there actually are errors in the Scriptures? How can Christ say that the man who continues in His Word shall know the truth? If the recorded Word of Christ is a grand mixture of truth and error, this is a very misleading promise. How is it possible for such a mixture of truth and error to make a man free? Obviously in the mind of Christ His Word was the truth. Later in His message Christ says to them, "But now ye seek to kill me, a man that hath told you the truth, which I have heard of God" (John 8:40). There is no legitimate interpretation that can make these words mean that the Lord was speaking to them both truth and falsehood.

The Lord Jesus sums up this train of thought by saying, "He that is of God heareth God's words: ye therefore hear them not, because ye are not of God" (John 8:47). Absolute truth is available to the genuine believer. The person who does not hear or recognize the authority of the Word of God shows that his heart is not right with God. The man who rejects the Word of God cannot know God. This saying of Christ sounds about as unyielding and arbitrary as anything He ever said. Plainly He is teaching that the man who refuses to recognize His Word as the Word of God has no part with God at all.

JOHN 10:35

In this passage our Lord is defending His own claim to be the divine Son of God. When the Jews charge Him with blasphemy, He answers them, "Is it not written in your law, I said, Ye are gods? If he called them gods, unto whom the word of God came, and the scripture cannot be broken; Say ye of him, whom the Father hath sanctified, and sent into the world, Thou blasphemest; because I said, I am the Son of God?" (John 10:34-36). The Lord is not arguing the inspiration of Scripture; He is arguing His own Deity. The statement "the Scripture cannot be broken" is an aside. It is spoken as a self-evident truth which is beyond question. The Lord Jesus certainly did not speak this in hypocrisy just to win an argument. He actually believed that the sacred Scripture could not be broken (or loosed from its power or authority.) This statement is a good indication of the true attitude of Christ toward the written Scriptures. In Christ's mind it was impossible for the Scripture to be broken.

JOHN 12:47-48

The Lord Jesus Christ came into the world to save sinners, not to judge the world. Because of this, Christ does not now judge the person who refuses to believe in Him, but that person will yet be judged. Here the Lord says, "He that rejecteth me, and receiveth not my words, hath one that judgeth him: the word that I have spoken, the same shall judge him in the last day" (John 12:48). This implies that His Word will be adequately recorded, and man will be responsible for its reception. The man who sneers at the "mistakes" recorded in Christ's words ought to ponder this passage, for one day he will have to face those words and to account for his attitude. If Christ's Words are to be the standard of judgment in the last day, there cannot be errors in them, because that judgment will be "in righteousness" (Acts 17:31). Any mixture of truth and falsehood would be an unworthy standard.

JOHN 16:13-14

When the Lord Jesus prophesies the coming of the Holy Spirit, He says, "Howbeit when he, the Spirit of truth, is come, he will guide you into all truth: for he shall not speak of himself; but whatsoever he shall hear, that shall he speak: and he will shew you things to come. He shall glorify me: for he shall receive of mine, and shall shew it unto you" (John 16:13-14). This saying of the Lord is the authentication for the coming New Testament Scriptures. It is a prophecy that the Holy Spirit of God will communicate new truth to the coming church, and that this truth will be the authentic revelation from Christ.

But if the coming Scriptures are to be a mixture of truth and falsehood, why does Christ call the Holy Spirit "the Spirit of truth?" This can only mean that what the Spirit will reveal contains no error; the Spirit's revelation is the truth. Beyond this, Christ promises that the Spirit of truth "will guide you into all truth." This is bitter irony if all the Spirit can do is to communicate some truth along with some error in the written Word of God. Certainly Christ means to teach that the Holy Spirit will communicate the truth and the truth alone, and that this truth will be an infallible and inerrant guide to the new church.

JOHN 17:8, 17, 20

This is the great high-priestly prayer of the Lord Jesus; here the Lord is communing in worship and fellowship with His Father. There can be no charge leveled against this prayer that Christ is accommodating Himself to the ignorance of the people. He was not speaking to the people at all; He was communing in loving reverence with God the Father. There can be no question about His accuracy. He prays, "I have given unto them the words which thou gavest me; and they have received them" (John 17:8). God the Father had revealed to His Son, not just thoughts, not just ideas, but also words. Those very words Christ had communicated to the disciples, and the disciples had received them. This shows that those Liberals who say that God's revelation was the Word of God when He communicated it, but that the people could not receive it as the true Word of God are mistaken. This passage contradicts this idea. The words which Christ had communicated the disciples had received.

The Lord Jesus continues praying by saying, "Sanctify them through thy truth: thy word is truth" (John 17:17). The Word of God not merely contains the truth; it is the truth. Remember that Christ is not preaching to an ignorant multitude; rather He is praying to the Father, who cannot be misinformed about anything. When God the Son tells God the Father that His Word is the truth, who dares to contradict Him? Man can only give humble thanks that such a priceless gift was granted to him.

The thought of Christ leaps forward to all succeeding generations; He is not praying just for the apostles but also for those who will believe on Him through their word. "Neither pray I for these alone, but for them also which shall believe on me through their word" (John 17:20). This means that Christ is taking thought for His Word as it will be recorded by the apostles for the benefit of coming generations. This means that every believer from that day to the end of time may comfort himself in the words of this prayer. If the Word of God was the truth in the first century world, it still is today.

ACTS 1:16

The apostle Peter speaks to the early disciples concerning Judas, saying, "Men and brethren, this scripture must needs have been fulfilled, which the Holy Ghost by the mouth of David spake before concerning Judas, which was guide to them that took Jesus" (Acts 1:16). This shows again that the apostles were in whole-hearted agreement with what the Old Testament prophets had said. The prophets had claimed that their words were the words of God. Peter agrees by saying, "the Holy Ghost spake by the mouth of David." The Holy Spirit was the originator of this prophecy; David was only the spokesman. (See also Acts 4:25; 28:25.)

ACTS 13:17-22, 29-30, 38-39

When the apostle Paul preaches this sermon in the synagogue of Pisidian Antioch, he uses the familiar style of a historical narrative. He describes how God has led the children of Israel out of Egypt in the Exodus, how He has endured their wilfulness in the wilderness wanderings, how God has driven the seven nations out of Canaan for the Israelites, how God has raised up for them the judges, Samuel the prophet, Saul the son of Kish, and David, the man after God's own heart. All of these are historical facts. The Liberals often raise the question of historical errors. They will sometimes say that although the doctrine in Scripture is true, there are many historical and factual errors in Scripture.

But in this sermon Paul is giving his approval to one account after another of the historical sections of the Old Testament. He names the persons and mentions the events of the Old Testament as history, not as legend. Can anyone conceive of the apostle Paul saying, "Perhaps some part of these recorded events may be true"? On the contrary, Paul recounts these historical events as the infallible Word of God just as he does the doctrinal passages.

If, however, these historical accounts are not inerrant, what about the later historical events in this sermon, when Paul speaks of the crucifixion and the resurrection (Acts 13:29-30)? If the historical facts of the Old Testament are just so many "myths" and "legends," what about those historical facts upon which the believer must base his salvation? Paul uses the same style in describing both sets of facts. Plainly the apostle Paul believes that both the historical and the doctrinal statements of Scripture are infallible and authoritative.

ACTS 20:32-35

On the last part of the third missionary journey Paul stops at Miletus to bid farewell to the Ephesian elders. He concludes his last message to them by saying, "And now, brethren, I commend you to God, and to the word of his grace, which is able to build you up, and to give you an inheritance among all them which are sanctified" (Acts 20:32). It is touching that Paul entrusts these men to God as he takes his leave of them, but the surprising thing is that he entrusts them to the word of His grace as well. If the Word that he left with them was a mixture of truth and falsehood, how could it build them up and give them an inheritance? Paul obviously regards that Word as the powerful and inerrant Word of God.

Paul encourages them to be steadfast and reminds them of the words of the Lord Jesus, "how he said, It is more blessed to give than to receive" (Acts 20:35). This is one of the sayings of the Lord which are not recorded in the Gospels, but Paul cites His spoken Word as just as authoritative and trustworthy as His recorded Word. Everything that the Lord Jesus said was infallible and inerrant, although not all that He said is necessary for man's salvation. What is necessary for man has been recorded in the Scriptures, and this we call *inspired,* but all that He said was inerrant.

ACTS 24:14

In this trial before the Roman governor, Felix, Paul is under obligation to tell the truth. He boldly confesses that he believes in the Lord Jesus, saying, "But this I confess unto thee, that after the way which they call heresy, so worship I the God of my fathers, believing all things which are written in the law and in the prophets" (Acts 24:14). This is not a hypocritical exaggeration; it is testimony in a court of law. Paul really did believe all the things which are recorded in the Old Testament Scriptures. The historical facts, the scientific facts, as well as the religious truths, were all zealously maintained by Paul. If the apostle Paul could say that he believed all that is written in the Scriptures, is not this the standard to which believers of today are also committed? But today many people who say this have mental reservations about how much they really will accept.

ROMANS 3:2

After Paul has proved that the Jew stands condemned before God just as the Gentile does, he inquires what advantage it was to be a Jew and answers, "Much every way: chiefly, because that unto them were committed the oracles of God" (Rom. 3:2). To the people of the first century world an oracle was a direct revelation of divine truth, a proclamation of the will of God. The primary advantage of the Jews was that to them were entrusted the Old Testament Scriptures, the oracles of God. The written Scriptures were not the opinions or prophecies of men; they were the inerrant revelation of the will of God. It is impossible for an oracle to be mistaken.

ROMANS 9:17

Although the formula "the Scripture saith" is a common way of citing absolute authority for the Jews, this passage is particularly significant in its use of these words. Paul says, "For the scripture saith unto Pharaoh, Even for this same purpose have I raised thee up, that I might shew my power in thee, and that my name might be declared throughout all the earth" (Rom. 9:17). The surprising thing about this is that in the passage which Paul is quoting, Ex. 9:16, it is God Himself who utters these words. This means that Paul is using the formula "Scripture saith" as synonymous with "God saith." The Scripture was so surely the infallible Word of God in Paul's mind that he could use the terms "Scripture saith" and "God saith" interchangeably. All the authority and trustworthiness of God Himself rested upon the written Word of Scripture.

I CORINTHIANS 2:13

Paul is teaching that the one who believes in the Lord Jesus has received, not the spirit of the world, but the Spirit of God, and therefore he has a capacity of spiritual understanding. Paul was certainly able to speak of "the deep things of God." But the genuine revelation which Paul proclaimed as the Word of God was not phrased in words which Paul had chosen, for he says,

"Which things also we speak, not in the words which man's wisdom teacheth, but which the Holy Ghost teacheth; comparing spiritual things with spiritual" (I Cor. 2:13). The letters which Paul wrote under inspiration were not the result of mere natural brilliance of mind and penetrating insight on Paul's part; they were the result of direct revelation by the Holy Spirit to Paul.

The Holy Spirit did not reveal just thoughts and concepts, but on the contrary He revealed the words in which the revelation of God was to be expressed. This does not mean that Paul became a mere machine. The Holy Spirit chose from Paul's vocabulary and style the exact expressions which would best convey the revelation of God and called them to Paul's mind. Therefore the letters of Paul were both the writings of an apostle and the infallible Word of the Living God. Although natural human wisdom may be mistaken, the wisdom which God communicates to His spokesmen can be neither false nor misleading. God will be true no matter what the response of man may be.

I CORINTHIANS 14:37

Paul was supremely confident that his words were the infallible Word of God. Although he struggled with controversial problems such as prophecy and speaking in tongues, he knew that he was faithful in giving the exact will of God in these matters. Therefore he says, "If any man think himself to be a prophet, or spiritual, let him acknowledge that the things that I write unto you are the commandments of the Lord" (I Cor. 14:37). A statement such as this manifests either sheer fanaticism, which does not fit Paul's character, or complete dedication to the guidance and control of God, which does fit Paul's character. Thus the first step for any man who considers himself spiritual is to admit that Paul wrote the authoritative Word of God. Any man who refuses to admit this is not a spiritual man in Paul's way of thinking. One cannot reject the writings of Paul and still enjoy the favor of God.

II CORINTHIANS 13:8

This complete commitment to the truth characterized Paul's whole manner of thinking. When his enemies impugned his character, he could say in all simplicity, "For we can do nothing against the truth, but for the truth" (II Cor. 13:8). Certainly Paul did not speak this hypocritically, because he was utterly dedicated to the truth. It is incredible that a man of Paul's character and worldwide testimony could be deceived as to the source and nature of his own writings. In the same way all the apostles were completely dedicated to the truth; they could not oppose it; they had to support it, because they were dedicated to God, who communicates only the truth. To say that the Scriptures are a mixture of truth and falsehood is to contradict pointedly the clear teaching of the apostles.

GALATIANS 1:8-12

Paul was so convinced of the infallibility of his message that he could say, "But though we, or an angel from heaven, preach any other gospel unto you than that which we have preached unto you, let him be accursed" (Gal. 1:8). This is the voice of a man who has proclaimed exactly what God has commanded him, who knows that his message is the infallible Word of God, and who believes that only the enemies of God will try to change or destroy that message. His sole purpose in life is to obey and to please the God who has commissioned him. Thus he can fling the challenge at his foes: ". . . do I seek to please men? for if I yet pleased men, I should not be the servant of Christ" (Gal. 1:10).

No man on earth could say that he had given Paul either his message or his authority. Paul could solemnly declare, "But I certify you, brethren, that the gospel which was preached of me is not after man. For I neither received it of man, neither was I taught it, but by the revelation of Jesus Christ" (Gal. 1:11-12). The Lord Jesus Christ revealed to Paul directly the Gospel and message which he was to proclaim. Could there be errors in this message? No! Paul would invoke a curse upon those who would try to change it. There was not a single error; there was not a single flaw in any part of Paul's message, because the responsibility for its truth lay with the Lord Jesus Christ. Paul had faithfully proclaimed His Word, and since He is the truth, there was no possibility of mistake. There can be no more earnest testimony to the inerrancy of the Scriptures than this steadfast conviction of the apostle Paul.

GALATIANS 3:16

Although Paul often uses the exact phraseology of the Old

Testament to prove his argument, no example is more striking than the present one. His whole argument stands or falls on the fact that the word *seed* is singular and not plural. Sometimes Liberals will sneer at this example as a "rabbinic" argument, because the word *seed* is a collective noun that may mean *descendants*. It is certain, however, that the word *seed* may refer to a single person, because Isaac is designated as the seed in Genesis 21:12. Paul is well aware that *seed* has a collective sense; indeed, in the same chapter he uses it in a collective sense: "If ye be Christ's, then are ye Abraham's seed" (Gal. 3:29).

Therefore Paul takes up this argument with full knowledge in order to establish the true meaning of the Old Testament passage. "Now to Abraham the promises were spoken, and to his seed. He saith not, And to the seeds, as of many; but as of one, And to thy seed, who is Christ" (Gal. 3:16).[1] Paul is clearly teaching that the Old Testament promise did not refer to the collective descendants of Abraham, but rather to the Messiah, the Lord Jesus Christ. The Lord is the fulfillment of this promise, and therefore the word *seed* had to be singular in form as well as in meaning. If the Old Testament had read *seeds*, it would have been a mistake, but this was not the case. In Paul's mind not only the vocabulary meaning, but even the form of the words of Scripture was divinely inerrant and authoritative.

EPHESIANS 1:13

Again and again in the writings of Paul, he refers to the final and absolute truth of his message. He refers to Christ by saying, "In whom ye also trusted, after that ye heard the word of truth, the gospel of your salvation" (Eph. 1:13). Because the Gospel which Paul has preached to them is the Word of truth, there could be no error in it, and they can trust it for their salvation with all assurance. It is highly questionable whether such serene faith could exist, if God's revelation, whether spoken or written, were a mixture of truth and error. The Lord Himself, not Paul, is responsible for the trustworthiness of the Scriptures.

I THESSALONIANS 2:13

Wherever Paul goes, he presents his message as the Word of God, and not as his own opinions or teachings. Thus he mentions to the Thessalonians his pleasure over their sincere reception of his preaching by saying, "For this cause also thank we God without ceasing, because, when ye received the word of God which ye heard of us, ye received it not as the word of man, but as it is in truth, the word of God, which effectually worketh also in you that believe" (I Thes. 2:13). For Paul there is always a sharp contrast between his message and the vain reasonings and speculations of men; his message is the infallible Word of the Living God. Because the Thessalonians have received his message as just this, he is rejoicing in their faith.

I TIMOTHY 4:1, 16

In the Pastoral Epistles the phrase *the faith* is often used in the sense of an objective revelation, whereas previously Paul has usually meant the subjective act of believing. This passage conveys a clearly objective sense as Paul says, "Now the Spirit saith expressly, that in the latter times some shall depart from the faith, giving heed to deceiving spirits and doctrines of demons" (I Tim. 4:1).[1] The phrase *the faith* in this statement certainly refers to the objective doctrine which Paul has taught and written. The person who departs from this standard of the faith is giving heed to the teaching of demons. Paul does not mince words concerning those who would disagree with the revelation which he proclaims.

It is interesting to note his statement, "the Spirit saith expressly." This was not the prophecy of Paul, but of the Holy Spirit. In addition, this was not just the general thought of the Spirit, but His express teaching on the matter. Thus Paul can exhort Timothy, "Take heed unto thyself, and unto the doctrine" (I Tim. 4:16). Since this doctrine was the inerrant Word of God, it was most appropriate for Timothy to give himself wholly to this doctrine.

I TIMOTHY 5:18

One of the most common ways of citing the Old Testament as an absolute authority was the New Testament expression, "the Scripture saith." In this passage the surprising thing is that after using the formula, "the Scripture saith," Paul quotes both the Old Testament and the New Testament Scriptures! He says, "For the Scripture saith, Thou shalt not muzzle the ox that treadeth out the corn. And, The labourer is worthy of his reward" (I Tim. 5:18). Thus Paul quotes from Deuteronomy 25:4 about not muzzling the ox, and, including it in the same formula, he quotes from Luke

10:7 about the laborer being worthy of his wages. This shows that Paul considered the New Testament to be on the same plane as the Old Testament and would quote them both as equally inerrant and authoritative.

II TIMOTHY 2:15, 25

In his last recorded letter to his faithful helper, Timothy, Paul exhorts him to give all diligence to the Word of God, saying, "Be ambitious to present thyself approved to God, a workman who does not need to be ashamed, cutting straight the Word of truth" (II Tim. 2:15).[1] The expression "cutting straight" probably refers to cutting out a straight road according to the image used in Hebrews 12:13 and in the Septuagint translation of Proverbs 11:5. Timothy is to mark out a straight path for himself and is not to use the Word of God crookedly. "The Word of truth" certainly refers to the written Scriptures which Timothy had in his own possession. Because the contents of the Word of truth are completely trustworthy and inerrant, the minister of Christ ought to handle them with care and faithfulness.

Paul keeps on maintaining that the Scriptures are the truth. He urges Timothy to use gentleness in correcting opponents, for perhaps God will grant them repentance that leads to the knowledge of the truth (II Tim. 2:25). This contradicts the Liberal claim that accurate knowledge of the truth is not possible for man in this life. In Paul's mind, the person who comes to surrender to the Lord Jesus Christ can know the truth.

II TIMOTHY 3:7, 15-17

When Paul warns Timothy that difficult times are coming in the last days, he makes clear that the difficulty will be with the character of man. One of about 22 characteristics of man apart from God that Paul mentions is that he is "ever learning, and never able to come to the knowledge of the truth" (II Tim. 3:7). This presupposes that there is an absolute knowledge of the truth which is available to mankind, but mere human learning is no substitute for the truth of God.

Paul reminds Timothy of the way his mother, Eunice, has instructed him, "and that from a child thou hast known the holy scriptures" (II Tim. 3:15). Because these sacred writings are able to impart the wisdom that leads to salvation through faith in

Christ, they are obviously a divinely authoritative and infallible guide. To say that the Scriptures are a mixture of truth and error is to contradict the clear teaching of the apostle.

Continuing his exhortation to Timothy, Paul says, "Every Scripture is God-breathed and profitable" (II Tim. 3:16).[1] In the Greek grammatical construction this phrase has two predicate adjectives which are connected by an *and*. Some Liberals would like to change one of these predicate adjectives to an attributive position so that it would read as the English Revised Version does, "Every scripture inspired of God is also profitable." This would allow some Scriptures to be not inspired, and hence not profitable. But this clearly violates the grammatical structure of the phrase, and these same translators do not so confuse this construction elsewhere. In I Timothy 4:4 the English Revisers carefully preserve the predicate position of the two adjectives: "For every creature of God is good, and nothing to be rejected." The three predicate adjectives in Hebrews 4:12 are also translated with accuracy: "For the word of God is living, and active, and sharper than any two-edged sword." They would not think of translating one of these as an attributive adjective to read, "The living word of God is also active." Apparently the reason that they so change the construction in II Timothy 3:16 is because of religious bias against the strong doctrine of inspiration which is there taught. Why else would the normal reading of a sentence be changed?

According to this statement by Paul every passage of Scripture is God-breathed and profitable. Since he has already equated both the Old and New Testaments, Paul is teaching that there is no part of either the Old Testament or the New Testament that is not God-breathed and profitable. Newport White even admits that "every Scripture" may mean "the whole of Scripture," after the analogy of a similar grammatical construction in Matthew 2:3, "the whole of Jerusalem."[3] Probably the best interpretation is "every single passage of Scripture."

The word which is usually translated "inspired" means literally "God-breathed." Thus God has breathed forth Scripture with the meaning which He intends to convey to mankind. If this word does not teach the absolute truthworthiness and authority of Scripture, what does it teach? In addition, every part of Scripture is profitable "for doctrine, for reproof, for correction, for training which is in righteousness" (II Tim. 3:16-17). This would not be the case if Scripture was partly truth and partly error, for then many passages would need correction, instead of being for correction. Inerrancy is demanded by the meaning of the sentence.

The purpose of Scripture is "that the man of God may be complete, having been thoroughly equipped for every good work" (II Tim. 3:17).[1] In Paul's mind the Scriptures are completely adequate for this purpose; therefore, there is nothing lacking in the Scriptures which is necessary for man. This means that when the New Testament Scriptures were completed, the canon of Scripture was closed. There is no other revelation from God which man needs; otherwise, man could not be "thoroughly equipped for every good work" by Scripture alone.

II TIMOTHY 4:2-4

In his concluding admonitions to Timothy, Paul charges him: "Preach the word; be instant in season, out of season; reprove, rebuke, exhort with all longsuffering and doctrine" (II Tim. 4:2). *The Word* obviously refers to the written Scriptures which he has just mentioned. Timothy can reprove and rebuke through preaching that Word because it is the Word of the Living God. There could not be a single error in it; the teaching of Scripture absolutely settles any doctrine and may be used to correct teaching from any other source.

As Paul continues, he warns Timothy that "the time will come when they will not endure sound doctrine" (II Tim. 4:3). In Paul's way of thinking this means the true Scriptural doctrine, for he adds, "They shall turn away their ears from the truth, and shall be turned unto fables" (II Tim. 4:4). Paul would never classify any part of Scripture as a "myth" or "fable." On the contrary, the Scripture is the "truth," and anyone who turns away to something else is turning away to a "fable."

TITUS 1:9, 14

When Paul writes to Titus, who was his representative on the island of Crete, he commands him to ordain elders in every city. He then gives Titus a list of qualifications to look for in selecting elders. The sixteenth qualification is that the elder ought to be "holding fast the faithful word as he hath been taught, that he may be able by sound doctrine both to exhort and to convince the gainsayers" (Tit. 1:9). "The faithful word" is the true Scriptural doctrine, the only one of which Paul would approve. If the Word is "faithful," it cannot have errors in it.

Later on Paul charges Titus not to give "heed to Jewish fables, and commandments of men, that turn from the truth" (Tit. 1:14). The Scripture is the truth; it is not merely the commandments of men. This high view of the Scripture was the consistent teaching of the apostle Paul. To him the Scripture was divinely infallible and authoritative.

HEBREWS 1:1, 6-8

The writer to the Hebrews fully shared this high view of the Scripture. In fact he could refer to God "who spoke to the fathers in the prophets" (Heb. 1:1).[1] This clearly teaches that the prophets were not responsible for their messages, but God was responsible. Even more surprising is his practice of quoting words which are spoken to or about God in the Old Testament, and saying "God saith." Thus he can say, "And again, when he bringeth in the first-begotten into the world, he saith, And let all the angels of God worship him" (Heb. 1:6). The antecedent of the word *he* in this passage must be God, but in the Septuagint translation of Deuteronomy 32:43, which he is quoting, it is Moses who is speaking these words. The writer to the Hebrews goes on to say, "And of the angels he saith, Who maketh his angels spirits, and his ministers a flame of fire" (Heb. 1:7). "He saith" must again refer to God, but in Psalm 104:4 it is the psalmist who is uttering these words.

This can only be because the writer to the Hebrews believed that the Scriptures were the voice of God. For him "Scripture saith" and "God saith" were convertible terms. The statements of Scripture carried the full authority of God. And from the way in which the writer to the Hebrews uses these terms, he certainly does not expect his readers to differ with him. This shows a long established habit of thought. In his mind whatever Scripture says is the revelation of the Living God.

HEBREWS 4:4

Again the writer to the Hebrews refers to God by saying, "For he spake in a certain place of the seventh day on this wise, And God did rest the seventh day from all his works" (Heb. 4:4). The *he* must refer to God, but if we consult Genesis 2:2, we find that this is the writer who is talking about God. Once again this is evidence that the writer to the Hebrews held that whatever the Scripture said was the infallible Word of God.

HEBREWS 5:12

In continuing his exhortation, the writer to the Hebrews re-proaches his readers for being dull in their reception of spiritual truth and adds, "For when for the time ye ought to be teachers, ye have need that one teach you again which be the first principles of the oracles of God; and are become such as have need of milk, and not of strong meat" (Heb. 5:12). Thus the writer is classifying God's revelation to man as the Oracles of God; "the Oracles of God" is equivalent to "the Scriptures." The whole ancient world acknowledged that an oracle was the revelation of the divine will. We have already seen that the apostle Paul has referred to the Scriptures as "the Oracles of God" (Rom. 3:2). This term pre-supposes inerrancy.

JAMES 1:18-22

When James, the Lord's brother, writes to the twelve tribes which are scattered abroad, he speaks of every good and perfect gift coming down from the Father. There is no variableness with the Father, for "of his own will begat he us with the word of truth" (Jas. 1:18). "The word of truth" refers to the Gospel which the apostles were preaching and writing. Paul makes a similar connection in I Corinthians 4:15. This Word of truth has supreme authority, because James charges his readers to lay aside all evil and to "receive with meekness the implanted word, which is able to save your souls" (Jas. 1:21).[1] The image is that of the parable of the sower, in which the seed is the Word which becomes rooted in the heart of the believer and brings forth fruit.

James sternly warns his readers, "but be ye doers of the word, and not hearers only, deceiving your own selves" (Jas. 1:22). This no doubt refers to the familiar Jewish custom of reading the Old Testament Scriptures every Sabbath day in the synagogues. Apparently the Christian church adopted this custom from earliest times (I Tim. 4:13). They were not to sit back and listen to the reading of the Scriptures and then to think that their obligations had ended; they were to practice the precepts of Scripture be-cause the Word of truth had the power to save their souls (Jas.

1:21). This also presupposes the divine trustworthiness and inerrancy of the Scriptures.

I PETER 1:10-12

It is clear that the Scripture writers are not giving their own opinions and messages, because sometimes they utter prophecies which they themselves do not understand. Peter mentions the Old Testament prophets who prophesied of the coming salvation in Christ, and he says, "Of which salvation the prophets have enquired and searched diligently, who prophesied of the grace that should come unto you: Searching what, or what manner of time the Spirit of Christ which was in them did signify, when it testified beforehand the sufferings of Christ, and the glory that should follow" (I Pet. 1:10-11). Plainly, the Holy Spirit moved the prophets to prophesy things concerning Christ which they did not fully understand even though they searched and enquired diligently. The Holy Spirit of God was responsible for the messages of the prophets, and He revealed to them that it was not for themselves that they prophesied but for succeeding generations (I Pet. 1:12).

Peter adds that now men are preaching the Gospel with the Holy Ghost sent down from heaven. The message of the Good News in Christ was not something worked up by man, but rather it was given by the Lord, and even its proclamation was empowered by the Holy Spirit. If there are mistakes in the prophecies which were written down, to whom shall they be attributed? Both the apostles and the prophets disown all responsibility. Shall modern man dare to attribute "mistakes" to God?

II PETER 1:19-21

Sometimes the Liberals complain about the lack of eyewitnesses for the miraculous events recorded in the Gospels, but here the apostle Peter gives his eyewitness testimony concerning the transfiguration. Peter solemnly declares that "we have not followed cunningly devised fables," but rather he describes his own eyewitness account of the events of the transfiguration (II Pet. 1:16-18). What is particularly surprising is Peter's conclusion: "We have also a more sure word of prophecy; whereunto ye do well that ye take heed, as unto a light that shineth in a dark place, until the day dawn, and the day star arise in your hearts" (II Pet. 1:19). Consider what Peter claims: The Word of prophecy is more sure than the voice of God speaking from heaven! Of course, it is the same voice whether written or spoken, but Peter claims that the prophetic Word is more trustworthy, more accurate, more permanent than the spoken voice of God, because the excitement of the occasion, the poor memories of those present might render the remembrance of the Words faulty. But the Word of God stands written: infallible, authoritative, and permanent.

Peter also gives a key for the understanding of Scripture. He says, "Knowing this first, that no prophecy of the scripture is of any private interpretation" (II Pet. 1:20). Thus no man can take a passage of the Scripture and can declare rightly what it means by his own personal judgment, if in doing this he disregards the teaching of the rest of Scripture. An individual passage of Scripture may be rightly interpreted by comparing its meaning with the harmonious teaching of the rest of Scripture. A man's personal opinion is not adequate for determining the meaning of Scripture, "for prophecy never was brought by the will of man, but men spoke from God, being borne along by the Holy Spirit" (II Pet. 1:21).[1] Since the Spirit of God gave the prophetic Word, the Spirit of God alone can give the true interpretation of the Word to man.

The human writers of Scripture were not free to choose whatever words they wished in proclaiming their messages; they were literally "being borne along by the Holy Spirit."[1] The term "being borne along" is the very term used in Acts 27:17 when the great storm caught Paul's ship on the voyage to Rome, and when they could not bear up against the wind, the seamen struck sail and so "were being borne along" by the wind. If this word means anything, it teaches that the Scripture writers were under the controlling power of the Holy Spirit and that they were not the masters of their own pens. This does not mean that they were mere robots, but the ultimate choice of their words was not their's but God's.

II Peter 3:15-16

The apostle Peter grew in grace as long as he lived, as this passage shows, for here Peter pays public tribute to the apostle Paul, who at one time had publicly rebuked Peter (Gal. 2:11). Peter writes, "And account that the longsuffering of our Lord is salvation; even as our beloved brother Paul also according to the wisdom given unto him hath written unto you; As also in all his epistles, speaking in them of these things; in which are some things hard to be understood, which they that are unlearned and unstable wrest, as they do also the other Scriptures, unto their own destruction" (II Pet. 3:15-16). This certainly was not spoken in hypocrisy; Peter, in all sincerity, calls him "our beloved brother Paul."

The important point in this passage, however, is that Peter puts all the epistles of Paul on the same plane as "the other Scriptures," which obviously means the Old Testament Scriptures which Christians and Jews alike revered. Clearly Peter regards both the Old Testament and the writings of Paul as "Scripture," and therefore authoritative and inerrant. Peter admits that there are "some things hard to be understood" in the writings of Paul, but the person who tries to twist Paul's writings merely shows himself to be "unlearned and unstable." This can only be because his writings are also the Word of the Living God, for the men who try to twist them do so "unto their own destruction."

I JOHN 4:6

To the apostle John all things are very clear: everything is either light or darkness, truth or error, from God or from the evil one. He could write statements that are strikingly simple, but their true depths can perhaps never be plumbed. In one such statement he says, "We are of God: he that knoweth God heareth us; he that is not of God heareth not us. Hereby know we the spirit of truth, and the spirit of error" (I John 4:6). This manifests staggering confidence; this is the voice of a mystic who has seen things and has heard things which only God could convey. If any man wishes to repudiate John's message, it certainly will not dismay John! He has the serene assurance that the Spirit of truth rests upon him, and the man who disagrees with him shows that he does not know God, but rather is possessed by the spirit of error. If we raise the question, "Did John think that his writings were a mixture of truth and error?" the answer is self-evident. For John, it is impossible to have the slightest error in the truth.

I JOHN 5:10-11

Simple faith in Christ as the divine Son of God is the great touchstone for the apostle John. As he says, "He that believeth on the Son of God hath the witness in himself: he that believeth not

God hath made him a liar; because he believeth not the record that God gave of his Son. And this is the record, that God hath given to us eternal life, and this life is in his Son" (I John 5:10-11). The person who does not believe the record which God gave concerning His Son is trying to make Him a liar, but then John goes on to tell exactly what that record is: God has given to us eternal life in His Son. If any man says that there is an error in that statement, John would charge that man with trying to make God a liar. There could hardly be a doctrine of inerrancy more sweeping than this. John, however, regards all his statements with the same calm assurance of infallibility.

II JOHN 1-10

John loves to hear that his converts are walking in the truth (vs. 4). The modern idea that truth is a relative thing never occurred to John, because he was supremely confident that a believer could know the truth (vs. 1). Thus John could label anyone who opposed his teaching as a "deceiver" (vs. 7). He adds, "whosoever transgresseth, and abideth not in the doctrine of Christ, hath not God" (vs. 9). For John, the doctrine was an absolute standard for which he would compromise nothing; therefore he says, "If there come any unto you, and bring not this doctrine, receive him not into your house, neither bid him God speed: For he that biddeth him God speed is partaker of his evil deeds" (vs. 10-11). Although John was the apostle of love, he was also the apostle of the truth. These two virtues do not conflict; they are both equally important.

JUDE 3

In this familiar passage Jude exhorts believers to "earnestly contend for the faith which was once-for-all delivered to the saints" (Jude 3).[1] Again the term "the faith" refers to the objective revelation of the Scriptures. The believer should earnestly contend for this faith; he should not sit by placidly while men tear down the trustworthiness and inerrancy of the revelation of God. This passage is further testimony that when the New Testament revelation was completed, the canon of the sacred Scripture was closed, for the faith was "once-for-all delivered to the saints." All the revelation which is necessary for man is to be found in the Scriptures.

REVELATION 2:7, 11, 17, 29; 3:6, 13, 22

Seven times over in the messages to the seven churches of Asia John says, "He that hath an ear, let him hear what the Spirit saith unto the churches" (Rev. 2:7). If John were giving his own thoughts and then saying that the Holy Spirit is saying them, these statements would have a hollow ring to them. At the least it would be deceitful; at the most it would be impious and blasphemous. John, however, was not giving his own words, but was faithfully writing the exact words which the Holy Spirit wanted recorded. The style and personality of John are apparent throughout his writings, but the power of the Holy Spirit resting upon John meant that his words would also be the words of the Living God.

REVELATION 22:18-19

As the book of the Revelation comes to a close, John says, "For I testify unto every man that heareth the words of the prophecy of this book, If any man shall add unto these things, God shall add unto him the plagues that are written in this book. And if any man shall take away from the words of the book of this prophecy, God shall take away his part out of the book of life, and out of the holy city, and from the things which are written in this book" (Rev. 22.18-19). The Liberals will patronizingly say that all "holy books" make some similar exaggerated claims of blessing and cursing. The fact remains, however, that it is the sacred Scripture that makes this claim. How are we to interpret this passage? If it is dangerous to add to or to take away from this book, does this not presuppose that this book is infallible and divinely authoritative? Why would it be wrong to take away the errors in a book? In this case it must be because there are none to remove. Other religious books may make similar claims, but no other book has similar ethical power and influence over the lives of modern thinking men. If the Scriptures are a unique book, its claims concerning itself deserve unique attention.

Thus we have briefly surveyed a few of the Scripture passages which bear upon the doctrine of the inspiration and inerrancy of the Scriptures. Although it has not been an exhaustive treatment, it is at least adequate to perceive what the harmonious teaching of Scripture on this doctrine is. The consistent teaching of all these passages has been that the Scriptures are divinely trustworthy, authoritative, and infallible. The personalities of the Scripture writers have not been obliterated, but at the same time the very words of the Living God have been faithfully transmitted by the inerrant inspiration of the Holy Spirit. This not a biased opinion forced upon Scripture; this is the consistent doctrine of Scripture concerning itself.

PART II

THE THEOLOGICAL VIEWS

Chapter III

THE HISTORIC FAITH OF THE CHURCH

The verbal inerrancy of Scripture has been the historic faith of the church in all ages. Some Liberal critics speak as though only a few "obscurantist Fundamentalists" would believe that Scripture is without error. On the contrary, scholarly believers from many different theological opinions in all periods of the church have treasured this faith in the Bible as the inerrant Word of God. From the many possible sources we will cite as representative examples three of the early church fathers, three of the reformers and founders of denominations, and three modern writers. Such a list could be extended indefinitely, and hence must be limited.

I. Testimony From the Fathers

When Clement of Rome wrote his First Epistle to the Corinthians, probably about A.D. 90-100, he said, "You have looked closely into the Holy Scriptures, which are given through the Holy Spirit. You know that nothing unrighteous or falsified has been written in them."[1] This is the testimony of the first generation after the apostles. They certainly recognized that they could not write with the infallibility of the Biblical writers.

In the following century Irenaeus, who died about A.D. 202, was equally decisive in teaching the inspiration and inerrancy of the Bible. He said that Christ "indicated in the clearest manner that the writings of Moses are His words. If then to Moses so also, beyond a doubt, the words of the other prophets are His."[2] In another work Irenaeus says very plainly, "It is unlawful to assert that the Scripture writers preached before they possessed perfect knowledge."[3] Such statements express the usual opinion of the early fathers.

Perhaps the best known of the church fathers is Augustine, A.D. 354-430. When he wrote to Jerome, Augustine said, "For I confess to your charity that I have learned to defer this respect and honor to those Scriptural books only which are now called canonical, that I believe most firmly that no one of those authors has erred in any respect in writing."[4] Of course, Augustine's influence on theological thought has been profound and continues to be felt. We must now leave the fathers. If the reader wishes further testimony from them, he may consult a comprehensive survey of the teachings of the fathers on the doctrine of inspiration in *An Introduction to the Study of the Gospels* by B. F. Westcott.[5]

II. Testimony From the Reformers

In the writings of the reformers we find the same belief in the inspiration and inerrancy of the Scriptures. On one occasion Martin Luther wrote, "When you read the words of Holy Scripture, you must realize that God is speaking them."[6] No one can question that this statement teaches Verbal Inspiration. In Luther's thinking, however, such inspiration demanded inerrancy, for in another place he states bluntly, "The Scriptures have never erred."[7] This unmistakable profession of faith is common in his writings.

Such a faith in the infallibility of Scripture was shared by John Calvin. In a famous passage in his *Institutes* Calvin wrote, "Between the apostles and their successors, however, there is, as I have stated, this difference: that the apostles were the certain and authentic scribes of the Holy Spirit, and therefore their writings are to be received as the oracles of God; but succeeding ministers have no other office than to teach what is revealed and recorded in the sacred Scriptures."[8] Thus Calvin perceived the vast difference between the divinely inspired writings of the apostles and the non-inspired writings of all who followed them.

Although Calvin certainly allowed full play for the personalities of the Biblical writers, he often referred to the Scriptures as dictated. In one place, speaking of the prophetic Word, he said, "To these likewise were added the histories, which were the productions of the prophets, but composed under the dictation of the Holy Spirit."[9] He conceded, however, that this would not be believed except by the internal testimony of the Holy Spirit in the heart of the believer.[10] Most conservative theologians of today would not use the term *dictated* because they do not wish to risk making the Scripture writers appear to be mere machines, which they obviously were not.

The impassioned spirit of John Wesley heartily agreed with this high view of the inspiration of the Bible. His comments on the value of the Scriptures are well known: "God Himself has condescended to teach me the way. . . . He hath written it down in a book. O give me that book! At any price, give me the book of God! I have it: here is knowledge enough for me. Let me be *a man of one book.*"[11] These are not the words of a man who is doubtful concerning the authority or trustworthiness of the Scriptures.

Even though Wesley was a man of great forbearance, he would not tolerate the idea that there were errors in the sacred Scriptures. On one occasion he wrote, "Nay, if there be any mistakes in the Bible, there may as well be a thousand. If there be one falsehood in that book, it did not come from the God of truth."[12] Obviously, he felt that because God is the Author of the Bible, it could not contain even one error. For the views of the English reformers see Philip Hughes.[13]

These reformers and founders of denominations should not be considered just as individuals, because their faith has been shared by millions of their followers. On the one hand Lutheran children for centuries have learned Luther's *Small Catechism*. The meaning of the answer to the tenth question is unmistakable: " 'By inspiration of God' means that God the Holy Ghost moved the holy men to write, and put into their minds, the very thoughts which they expressed and the very words which they wrote (Verbal Inspiration)." The answer to the next question, "Whose word, then, is every word of the Bible?" is equally clear: "Every word of the Bible is God's word, and therefore the Bible is without error."[14] This is the historic faith of the Lutheran Church.

On the other hand the *Westminster Confession of Faith* has been the testimony of millions of the followers of Calvin. The first chapter states, "The authority of the Holy Scripture, for which it ought to be believed and obeyed, dependeth not upon the testimony of any man or church, but wholly upon God (who is truth itself), the author thereof; and therefore it is to be received, because it is the Word of God."[15]

One commentator on this article has said, "The ultimate authority of Holy Scripture is declared to rest upon God Himself, from whom it comes. His Spirit inspires it, and this renders it infallible."[16] The Westminster Confession adds, however, that "our full persuasion and assurance of the infallible truth, and divine authority thereof, is from the inward work of the Holy Spirit, bearing witness by and with the word in our hearts."[17] Those people, consequently, who have not experienced the gracious work of the Holy Spirit of God are not expected to share this faith.

III.   Testimony From Modern Writers

It should not be thought that this clear faith was possible only in past centuries. The inspiration and inerrancy of Scripture is still the steadfast faith of many devout Christian scholars. A modern Lutheran scholar, T. E. Engelder, testified in 1944, "To those who would entice us away from an inerrant Bible we give this answer: No Christian can declare, in his sober mind, that God's Word contains errors. And when the Christian realizes that Scripture *is* God's Word, he cannot, absolutely he cannot, declare that the Holy Scriptures contain errors."[18] Obviously, Engelder feels that it is incompatible with the nature of God to mix error with the truth which God reveals. Is not this a valid and cogent argument?

Another faithful witness is Edward J. Young, a Reformed scholar, who taught at Westminster Theological Seminary (Philadelphia). In 1957 he wrote, "The Bible is inerrant. That Word which the Holy God gave to man is a Word that in all its statements is to be trusted. Upon its utterances we may fashion our lives and actions."[19] Every converted Christian who has experienced the transforming power of the Word of God in his life can agree with such a testimony. It strikes a responsive chord in the born-again heart.

In a recent reference work (1964) Johannes Vos spoke of the work of the Holy Spirit in directing the Biblical writers. "This influence of the Holy Spirit so guided and controlled the Biblical writers that the product of their writing was exactly what God intended and free from errors of every kind. Because of this, the Bible is called the infallible or inerrant Word of God."[20] This theologically exact definition is the historic faith of the church.

The Christian who trusts in the Word of the Lord Jesus Christ for his salvation does not find it difficult to accept His Word concerning the inerrancy of Scripture (Matt. 5:17-18). This simple faith is the heritage of a mighty company of true followers of the Lord in all ages. Those who put their trust in the Word of Christ will never be put to shame, but those who refuse to believe in Christ's estimate of the sacred Scriptures ought to realize that they have departed from the historic faith of the church.

COMPARISON OF THEOLOGICAL VIEWS ON INSPIRATION[1]

	LIBERALISM	NEO-ORTHODOXY	NEO-EVANGELICALISM	STRICT CONSERVATISM
1. The relationship between the Bible and modern religious thought.	1. Modern religious thought is all-important. Let's salvage from the Bible what we can.	1. The Bible is authoritative and necessary. Let's incorporate into it all the modern religious thought we can.	1. The Bible is all-important. But let's listen to modern religious thought and modify our view of the Bible where needed.	1. The Bible is all-important. Modern religious thought has value only when it agrees with Bible teaching. (II Cor. 10:5.)
2. Inspiration.	2. The Bible is inspired the same way that Shakespeare's writings are.	2. The passages of the Bible in which you encounter God are inspired; the rest are not.	2. The Bible is divinely inspired in a unique sense.	2. The Bible is divinely inspired in a unique sense. (II Tim. 3:16.)
3. Inerrancy.	3. The Bible is full of errors.	3. The Bible is full of errors.	3. The Bible may contain some errors, even in the original manuscripts.	3. The Bible in the original manuscripts did not have one error. (Matt. 5:17-18.)

[1]The author is aware that some men will not fit this simple classification, but such responses are typical of these respective views.

CHAPTER IV

THE LIBERAL VIEW OF INSPIRATION

The modern Liberal movement draws directly on the work of the German theologian Schleiermacher. More than a century ago he taught that the true source of theology was not the Bible, but man's religious consciousness. Thus the objective revelation of God in the Bible was set aside, and man's subjective opinions were exalted to the position of authority. Schleiermacher argues at length that nothing should be accepted just because it occurs in the Bible. Even though he would accept some things in Scripture, it would be because they agree with his previous opinions, and even then he adds, ". . . if precautions be taken to avoid the impression that a doctrine must belong to Christianity because it is contained in Scripture, whereas in point of fact it is only contained in Scripture because it belongs to Christianity."[1] In other words, man decides what belongs in Christianity. If part of the Bible agrees with his opinions, he accepts it; if part disagrees, he is free to throw it out.

I. DIRECT ATTACK

Man's natural religious insight is to decide what is correct and what is not. The most outspoken advocate of this view in modern times was Harry Emerson Fosdick. Although he purported to teach others the value of the Bible, he led the attack on the inspiration of the Scriptures. In one work he refers to the doctrine of inspiration by saying, "So we used to think of inspiration as a procedure which produced a book guaranteed in all its parts against error, and containing from beginning to end a unanimous system of truth. No well-instructed mind, I think, can hold that now."[2] Here again the mind of man is the standard of judgment; this agrees very well with the old German school of Rationalism.

Fosdick had a natural explanation ready for most of the supernatural events in Scripture. He would categorically deny miracle after miracle; for example, in one work he said, "The miraculous aspects of the plagues in Egypt and the magic fall of Jericho's walls may be legendary heightenings of historical events; the amazing tales of Elijah and Elisha may be largely folklore; and, in the New Testament, finding a coin in a fish's mouth to pay the temple tax, or walking on water, or blasting a tree with a curse, may be just such stories as always have been associated with an era of outstanding personalities and creative spiritual power. Certainly, I find some of the miracle-narrative of Scripture historically incredible."[3] In this manner he mounted a frontal assault on the trustworthiness and authority of the Bible.

II. INDIRECT METHODS

Most modern Liberal writers adopt a more sophisticated and subtle kind of phraseology, although recently (1963) Henry P. Van Dusen, formerly president of Union Theological Seminary (New York), singled out the Creed of Chalcedon for some degree of scorn because it referred to Christ as "God truly and man truly," by saying, "To the logical mind, it sounds like distilled nonsense."[4] Once again the mind of man is the only authority. Later, Van Dusen asked plaintively, "Where lies the norm for the discrimination of truth from error, of the enduring from the transient, of authentic Christian Truth from its imperfect anticipations and its illegitimate elaborations?"[5] If the natural mind of man must decide all this, it remains a most perplexing subjective problem.

A typically subtle line of attack is Rudolf Bultmann's attempt to "de-mythologize" Scripture. Because Bultmann is convinced that Scripture is filled with "myths," he is attempting to destroy the historical facts of the Scripture by citing all the "myths" which have encrusted the events recorded. In referring to the historical person, Jesus Christ, Bultmann wrote, "His person is viewed in the light of mythology when he is said to have been begotten of the Holy Spirit and born of a virgin, and this becomes clearer still in Hellenistic Christian communities where he is understood to be the Son of God in a metaphysical sense, a great, pre-existent heavenly being who became man for the sake of our redemption and took on himself suffering, even the suffering of the cross. It is evident that such conceptions are mythological. . . ."[6] Such a statement also makes it evident that Bultmann has thrown out the entire supernatural character of Christ and has reduced Him to a mere natural human being. If this is all that is left of the Person of the Lord Jesus Christ, certainly we cannot expect Bultmann to be any more merciful toward the Bible itself. His own intellect is clearly the only standard by which Bultmann is judging everything.

The Liberals cannot seem to understand that there is something higher than the mind of man: namely, God's revelation embodied in the Scriptures. If man were the highest personality in existence, we could understand his pride of mind, but if we grant the existence of God, there can be no discredit to man in receiving from God the revelation of truths which he could not otherwise know. There is nothing degrading in acknowledging the fact that God's wisdom is higher than our wisdom, and that every thought should be brought into captivity to God.

God does not expect man to abandon his reason, but He does expect man to bring his reason into obedience to the revealed will of God (Rom. 12:2; II Cor. 10:5). Because the Liberals have ignored the sinful nature of man, they have exalted the human mind to a place of authority which rightfully belongs only to God. A former Liberal who is now Neo-Orthodox, Reinhold Niebuhr, has criticized Liberalism on this very point: "The real basis for all the errors of Liberalism is its erroneous estimate of human nature."[7] This critical statement does not mean that Niebuhr has abandoned all of his Liberalism, for "the fundamental problems which Niebuhr sets out to solve are the characteristic problems of Liberalism: the discovery of the meaning of the Bible beyond a literalistic orthodoxy, the establishment of the practice of tolerance, the relating of the Gospel to cultural movements and the search for its intelligibility in relation to human experience."[8] If the Bible does not mean what it says, then it is difficult indeed to discover its true meaning. A disastrous flaw in all man-made systems of reasoning is their failure to believe God's revelation in Scripture; they cannot attain eternal reality apart from His revelation. Simple faith in the revealed Word of God is the necessary foundation for all valid Christian thought.

III. SYMBOLIC INTERPRETATION

The Liberals consistently attack any acceptance of the literal statements of the Bible; they prefer to give a symbolic meaning to the Scriptures. L. Harold DeWolf, professor of systematic theology, Wesley Theological Seminary (Washington, D.C.), has set forth the usual Liberal arguments for this position by saying, "The insistence of some conservative Christians on a Biblical literalism that is rationally indefensible and an appeal based on the 'proofs' of prophecy and miracles, in defiance of the natural sciences and the new historical understanding of Biblical times, needlessly drives from the Christian faith intelligent young people who will not blind themselves to scientific and historical evidences."[9]

In reality, no intelligent conservative Christian wishes to ignore scientific or historical facts, but when such facts are used to discredit Scripture, he is suspicious of them. For the believer there is no contradiction between God's Word, the Bible, and God's creation. Any alleged contradictions result from man's lack of understanding.

When DeWolf sneered at the "morally unworthy passages" and referred to "the portrayals of a narrowly nationalistic and bloodthirsty God in Judges, Nahum and elsewhere,"[10] he simply showed his own lack of understanding. There are many things recorded in Scripture that are not meant for us to follow. The Bible expressly speaks with disapproval concerning the times of the Judges, when "every man did that which was right in his own eyes" (Judges 17:6). Even in this time of limited light God accepted men of genuine faith, but their actions are obviously not meant to be morally binding on later generations who have greater light and also greater responsibility.

The Bible may certainly quote the words and may describe the actions of Satan and evil men without thereby giving approval to such words and deeds. The Bible is the Word of God, not only because it gives us precepts to follow, but also because it gives us examples which we are not to follow. Although the Bible says, "There is no God," no intelligent Christian would claim that the Bible intends us to believe this. The context makes clear that the only man who believes such a thing is a fool. Thus the Word of God, the Bible, is a book of warning as well as a book of positive precepts.

But for many of the Liberals the term *Word of God* has a highly symbolic character. It does not refer to the Bible at all; hence, Paul Tillich can claim that the term *Word of God* should always have quotation marks around it. In a contribution to an anthology he wrote, "For if we leave out the quotation marks, we may encourage the idea that God has a language of his own and that the holy writings of religion are translations of the divine words into the words of a human dialect. Or if such an absurdity is avoided, it is still possible to insist that there are circumscribed places in man's oral and written traditions where the 'Word of God' may be found to the exclusion of all other places. An example of this instance can be seen in theological fundamentalism and primitive Biblicism where the sum of words contained between the two covers of a book is identified with the 'Word of God.' "[11]

According to Tillich, everything that any one says about God must have a highly symbolic character. This would include everything that is found in the Bible. Therefore any literal interpretation of Scripture would, according to him, be a misinterpretation.

Tillich singled out a particular phrase that is often heard in conservative churches, and said, "In some church services the minister concludes his reading of the Bible with the sentence, 'May God bless this reading of His holy Word.' For a thoughtful congregation, nothing could be more misleading than this sentence, for it identifies the 'Word of God' with the Scripture. It reduces the different meanings of 'Word of God' to one, and it blurs the difference between the divine Word given to the prophets and apostles in their state of inspiration and the human words in which they expressed their ecstatic experience. The Biblical words are human words. . . ."[12]

Thus he reasoned that what God spoke to the prophets was the inspired "Word of God" to them, but when they in turn spoke His Word to others, they could speak only fallible, human words. If this be true, it would mean that all the times that the prophets used the formula, "Thus saith the Lord" (Isa. 30:15; 37:6; 38:5; 43:1; 44:2; 52:3; and numerous others), the prophet was only witnessing to what God had said and was not giving the true "Word of God." This is certainly not consistent with either the words of the prophets or the historic faith of the church.

The conservative Christian has put his trust in the Word of God, meaning the Bible. He is not steeped in doubt as to what part of the Bible is inspired and what part is not; he believes the testimony of the Scripture itself as to its own inspiration and inerrancy. Even the Neo-Orthodox writer, Emil Brunner, admitted that Scripture itself started this identification of the "Word of God" with doctrine, for this is clearly taught in II Timothy 3:16.[13]

Brunner, however, would not regard the Pastoral Epistles as authentically Pauline.

Therefore the conservative believer should recognize that these men have departed from the historic faith of the church and should not let their unbelief trouble him. Since these men have repudiated the Person as well as the Word of the Lord Jesus Christ, it is ironic that they still claim the name "Christian." The believer who trusts in the Word of the Lord Jesus Christ for his salvation (Matt. 11:28 John 6:47) may do so with the confidence that he is trusting in the inspired and inerrant Word of God (John 14:26). Those who doubt the authority and inerrancy of those Words should remember that those very Words shall judge them in the last day (John 12:48).

CHAPTER V

THE NEO-ORTHODOX VIEW OF INSPIRATION

Many conservative Christians make the mistake of thinking that Neo-Orthodoxy is just another name for the old Liberalism. In reality there is a distinct difference. Liberalism is a frontal assault upon practically every important doctrine of the Christian faith, whereas Neo-Orthodoxy will outwardly agree with a great many of the major doctrines. Consequently, the points of disagreement must be carefully examined; the doctrine of inspiration is in the forefront of these contested points.

I. THE BIBLE IS WITNESS

Although the Neo-Orthodox sounds conservative when he stresses the value and importance of the Bible, he does not mean the same thing that the conservative means by these words. The conservative holds that the Bible is God's revelation; the Neo-Orthodox holds that it is not God's revelation, but rather the witness to the revelation. He makes such a distinction because he thinks that God cannot reveal Himself in a body of truth like the Bible, but rather reveals Himself in events like the crucifixion. This makes the Bible a record or witness of the revelation.

This is why Karl Barth can refer to the Bible by saying: "It witnesses to a revelation from God, but that does not mean that God's revelation is now before us in any kind of inherent quality of being divinely revealed. The Bible is not a book of oracles; it is not an instrument of direct impartation. It is really witness."[1] Barth also makes clear that the Bible is a very human witness, shot through with errors. He claims that "at every point it is the vulnerable word of man."[2] The prophets and apostles were actually "fallible, erring men like ourselves."[3] In fact, Barth stresses the earthly, Jewish character of the Scriptures: "The Bible as the wit-

74

ness of divine revelation is in its humanity a product of the Israelitish, or to put it more clearly, the Jewish spirit. . . . And we may well ask whether all the other offences which we may take at the Bible, and will necessarily take if we are without faith, are not trifles compared with this offence."[4] Barth does not encourage anti-Semitism, of course, but we can see by his phraseology what a low view he takes of Scripture. He maintains bluntly that "the prophets and apostles as such, even in their office, even in their function as witnesses, even in the act of writing down their witness, were real, historical men as we are, and therefore sinful in their action, and capable and actually guilty of error in their spoken and written word."[5]

The illustration that the Neo-Orthodox usually gives is that the Bible is like a minister preaching the Gospel. Although there may be many mistakes in his sermon, he is still witnessing to the truth, and this is sufficient to secure salvation for men. In the same way, the Neo-Orthodox say, the Bible is full of errors, and yet it witnesses to the truth and is therefore "adequate" for man.

No conservative would agree that this is an accurate portrayal of the value and importance of the Bible. The writings of the Non Orthodox are often obscure, but on this point they are exceedingly clear. Emil Brunner has written: "The orthodox doctrine of Verbal Inspiration has been finally destroyed."[6] In another work he charges that the Bible "is full of errors, contradictions, erroneous opinions concerning all kinds of human, natural, historical situations. . . . It is overgrown with legendary material even in the New Testament."[7] Thus he concludes: "A legalistic, immutable authority, such as the human desire for security would gladly possess — and indeed is offered in an orthodox doctrine of the Scriptures as an axiomatic authority, or in the Catholic doctrine of the infallible doctrinal authority of the Pope — is thus denied to us. The word of Scripture is not the final court of appeal. . . ."[8]

Specifically, the Neo-Orthodox doubt the authenticity of the words of Jesus which are recorded in the New Testament. Thus C. H. Dodd writes: "We no longer accept a saying as authoritative because it lies before us as a word of Jesus."[9] This basic doubt concerning what the average Christian would regard as a precious part of the Word of God is characteristic of the Neo-Orthodox position on the inspiration of the Bible. The conservative treasures the Bible as revealing the express commands of God on doctrine and practice, but Brunner is so doubtful about Scripture that he writes that "a final resort to a single Scriptural passage is impossible for us."[10]

II. MAN IS THE MEASURE

Whenever man denies that the Bible is God's authoritative revelation, he must substitute his own human reason as the final authority. Neo-Orthodoxy has made the mind of man the governing authority in ascertaining all truth. If, in reading the Bible, a part of it strikes a man as inspired, it is inspired; if it does not strike him as inspired, it is not inspired. Thus Neo-Orthodoxy has made the mind of man the standard for everything. This means that the Word of God is a subjective experience and not an objective revelation.

It is because of this overemphasis on the mind of man that C. H. Dodd can say concerning Romans, "Sometimes I think Paul is wrong, and I have ventured to say so. In the main, what he says seems to me to be profoundly true."[11] Dodd's own understanding will determine whether the Bible is true or not. If it does not seem to him to be true, he has no hesitation about rejecting it. Thus he can say bluntly, "Adam is a myth (though for Paul he *may* have been real)."[12] This is ultimately what Barth means when he comments on the same passage (Rom. 5:12), "Adam has no existence on the plane of history."[13] If a Biblical personality is not historical, certainly he must be mythological.

III. THE DEVIL IS NOTHINGNESS

One of the great flaws in Barth's theological system is the absence of the powers of evil. Since he cannot believe in the Scriptural teaching concerning the existence of the devil and demons, the struggle in the world must be between God and man alone. When he raises the question of the origin and nature of the devil and demons, he can only say that "their origin and nature lie in nothingness. . . . They themselves are always nothingness."[14] It does not seem to disturb him that Scripture teaches something altogether different. In fact, he can refer to Jude 6 and II Peter 2:4 on the fall of angels and mention the "intolerable artificiality with which attempts have been made to use them as a basis for the development of the doctrine of a fall of angels and therefore of an explanation of the existence of the devil and demons."[15] But one cannot set forth the teaching of Scripture fully without acknowledging the existence of a theme as important as the nature of the evil powers that have enslaved fallen man. This is why one theologian can complain, "Barth has the ability to a very large degree of being able to employ the language of Scripture in a system that is totally foreign to the Bible."[16]

The Neo-Orthodox theologians take some pains to refute the doctrine of the verbal inerrancy of Scripture because its acceptance would destroy their position. In this vein Barth says concerning the writers of Scripture, "To the bold postulate that if their word is to be the Word of God they must be inerrant in every word, we oppose the even bolder assertion, that according to the Scriptural witness about man, which applies to them too, they can be at fault in any word, and have been at fault in every word, and yet according to the same Scriptural witness, being justified and sanctified by grace alone, they have still spoken the Word of God in their fallible and erring human word."[17] Thus Barth is not afraid to oppose Scriptural doctrine at every point.

IV. NEO-ORTHODOXY IS ANTHROPOLOGY

Hordern advances a peculiarly philosophical objection to inerrancy. In his words, "An objective revelation is not inerrant until it is inerrantly received. The subjective receiver of revelation is an indispensable link in the chain. As Kierkegaard put it, there is no truth until there is truth to me. If there is to be inerrant revelation of propositions, the hearer would have to be as inerrant as the speaker."[18] But this is tantamount to saying that God would not be true unless man were there to prove it! God's character does not so change. God is true regardless of man's perception of it, and God's revelation is true regardless of man's reception of it. Barth's stress on man's reception of God's revelation has made his view a man-centered theology — one might almost call it an anthropology instead of a theology. Despite his protestations that he is attempting to restore God to the center of Christianity, Barth has not succeeded in his own system.

Thus the result of such a system is that man is his own authority; God is important only as man thinks so. These Neo-Orthodox presuppositions, however, destroy the heart of Christianity. If there is no objective authority in Christianity, how can the average Christian come to know the will of God for his life? Or, indeed, how can a Neo-Orthodox theologian believe that his own mind is the standard for all understanding of God? Why should a man listen to him rather than to another? Every man's mind becomes his own authority. Some of the Neo-Orthodox theologians are keenly aware of this problem. P. T. Forsyth said, "The peril of the hour is a religious subjectivism which is gliding down into religious decadence for want of an objective authority."[19]

How much better is the serene faith which the apostle John manifested when he wrote, "I have not written unto you because ye know not the truth, but because ye know it, and that no lie is of the truth" (I John 2:21). It is characteristic of John to maintain that there is an absolute objective standard of truth, and that men can come to know it. In the great High-priestly prayer our Lord prays for His own, "Sanctify them through thy truth: thy word is truth" (John 17:17). The one who believes in the Lord Jesus Christ may yet rest his faith in confidence of the fulfillment of that prayer.

CHAPTER VI

THE NEO-EVANGELICAL VIEW OF INSPIRATION

One of the outstanding characteristics of Neo-Evangelicalism is its questioning of the verbal inerrancy of Scripture. Consequently the advocates wish to "re-think" all the basic Christian doctrines in the light of what Liberal thinkers have said about them. This can lead to a modification of Christian doctrine solely on the basis of the changing philosophies of men. Their eagerness for intellectual prestige prompts them to make sweeping concessions to almost all theories of science, particularly that of organic evolution. They zealously advocate the cause of the ecumenical movement, and usually they have some harsh words to say about Fundamentalism.

I. ATTACK ON INERRANCY

The rising volume of questions can only be interpreted as an attack on the doctrine of inerrancy. Typical of the way the New Evangelicals question the inerrancy of Scripture is the statement by Edward John Carnell, "Orthodoxy may never officially decide whether the Holy Spirit corrected the documents from which the Chronicler drew his information."[1] This means that the writer of the Book of Chronicles may have quoted genealogies that had errors in them; he just quoted the errors accurately! The strict Conservative — one who believes in verbal inerrancy — would say that the Biblical writers were preserved from selecting erroneous material whatever source the writer used. The Holy Spirit guided them in choosing only what was true in fact as well as in doctrine.

Even Liberal scholars like L. Harold DeWolf comment: "It is noteworthy that Dr. Edward John Carnell has changed his theological position recently, so that he no longer defends the inerrancy of the original biblical manuscripts. . . ."[2]

Another one who claims to be a New Evangelical, Daniel

79

Stevick, in a recent work (1964) has argued at some length that the Bible itself cannot prove inerrancy. When he refers to that claim in Revelation 22:18-19 ("If any man shall take away from the words of the book of this prophecy. . . ."), he seems to treat the Bible as he would any other apocalyptic book, and asks with some degree of scorn, "In what sense does one establish the inerrancy of a statement about a beast with seven heads and ten horns?"[3] This does not sound like a man who regards the prophetic Word very highly.

Consequently, the result of this attitude of irreverence is that, according to Stevick, man himself must decide what part of the Bible is inerrant and what part is erroneous. It is obvious that Stevick has already decided against a good many passages in the Bible. In one place he says: "If the barbarous ethics of Judges or the imprecatory 'hate songs' in the Psalter or a vindictive vision in Revelation seems remote from, or even opposed to, the emerging Gospel, we need not defend any of them."[4]

This tendency to throw out passages in Scripture is actually the same practice to which Neo-Orthodoxy has come. These passages in Judges, Psalms, or Revelation do not strike Stevick as inspired, and since he cannot defend them, he is willing to abandon them. But perhaps the part of his book which manifests his attitude most clearly is the list of Selected Readings with which it closes. He dispatches the Conservatives with one curt statement; then with loving care he lists by author and title the works that he thinks are really valuable. This list is filled with Neo-Orthodox and Liberal men: C. H. Dodd, Baillie, Barth, Brunner, Forsyth, Niebuhr, Tillich, and many others. Apparently these men are his heroes.

II. Acceptance of Pseudonymity

Another serious question which has been raised by Bernard Ramm is pseudonymity. After citing James Orr's old contention that the Biblical writers did not sign someone else's name to deceive, he goes on to state, "But if pseudonymity were a recognized form in the culture of the scriptural writer, and if this would cause no offense to the people of that time, then we must be prepared to accept this as a proper form of special revelation."[5] As Ramm explains in a footnote, some scholars hold that Paul had a college of fellows and assistants who wrote his letters (such as the Pastoral Epistles) under Paul's signature. Although Ramm is careful to cite other scholars as holding these views of pseudonymity, apparently these ideas are congenial to his own thought.

But it is difficult to see how a companion or assistant to Paul could say in good conscience that his readers knew the persecutions which he endured at Antioch, Iconium, and Lystra (II Tim. 3:11). Unless this is Paul himself, it sounds hypocritical. In the same way, how could an assistant cry out in triumph, "I have fought a good fight, I have finished my course, I have kept the faith" (II Tim. 4:7)? The only adequate explanation of these passages is that the apostle Paul was indeed immediately responsible for the wording of these Epistles. The name with which they begin is the name of the one whose words fill the chapters which follow. If the Pastoral Epistles are rejected on the basis of pseudonymity, where shall the line be drawn as to which Epistles are considered genuine letters written by the one whose name they bear? Must we also discard Ephesians? Colossians? Jude? I and II Peter? What about Matthew? The Johannine writings? Is there a stopping place?

III. EMPHASIS ON LOVE, NOT DOCTRINE

It is characteristic of the New Evangelicals to stress that love, not doctrine, is of primary importance for the Christian.[6] Although they like to remind Fundamentalists that Scripture (I Cor. 13) exalts love above faith and knowledge, they seem unaware that Scripture does not exalt love above the truth. The mark of the disciple is not only love, but also continuing in the Word of Christ (John 8:31; 14:23). Any departure from the truth is wrong as is departure from love.

This matter of love is not consistently applied. It is all right to exercise love toward the Neo-Orthodox, but apparently it is also all right to forget about it when mentioning Fundamentalism!

Occasionally one detects an acid tone in the words of Carnell. He goes out of his way to demonstrate the poor mentality and boorishness of Fundamentalists. For the Fundamentalist "handing out tracts is much more important than founding a hospital. As a result, unbelievers are often more sensitive to mercy, and bear a heavier load of justice, than those who come in the name of Christ. The fundamentalist is not disturbed by this, of course, for he is busy painting 'Jesus Saves' on rocks in a public park."[7]

IV. EMPHASIS ON SCIENTIFIC THEORY

Another important aspect of the New Evangelicalism is its overpowering regard for scientific theory. Although no Christian should have any complaint with the facts of science, the believer should object when the theories of science contradict the clear teaching of Scripture. In particular, scientists have written much on the theories of origins.

The origin of the Solar System or of the universe is an event which was not observed by man, cannot be repeated, and in no way could its method be proved. Since Scripture has some definite statements on this subject, it is not unreasonable for the believer to maintain the trustworthiness of the Scriptural account of creation in contradiction to any scientific theory of origins. This does not mean that a conservative theory of origins, such as the "Gap theory" or the "24 hour day theory," is therefore correct. Any or all theories may be mistaken. What the Conservative must maintain is that the Scriptural account is without error.

The New Evangelicals, however, seem to favor the side of science in any contradiction with Scripture. Bernard Ramm has stated the New Evangelical position succinctly: "If the differences between the sciences and the Bible were to grow to a very large number and were of the most serious nature, it would be questionable if we could retain faith in Scripture."[8] This implies that where there is a serious contradiction between what science teaches and what Scripture teaches, the New Evangelicals will ultimately choose the side of science.

This is not the view of historic conservative Christianity. There should be no contradiction between the facts of science and the teaching of Scripture, but when men claim there is, the Christian should choose the side of Scripture. Science is continually changing, whereas God's revelation is not. As the Psalmist put it, "Forever, O Lord, thy word is settled in heaven" (Ps. 119:89).

There is a difference between science and scientism. In the realms which can be investigated and tested – the physical and biological realms – science has a legitimate and helpful task of explaining phenomena. All too often, however, a scientist who knows well a physical or biological science will assume that he is also an expert in religion or philosophy. This attitude that science has the answer in every field can well be called "scientism." But an individual scientist's opinion on the origin of the universe or the existence of God is no more certain than the opinion of any other man. The only sure illumination that man has in these areas is the revealed Word of God, the Bible.

Now it is clear that the New Evangelicals are willing to give the benefit of the doubt to the critics of Scripture and to the theories of men rather than to the Bible itself. It is strange that these men accuse conservatives of *hyperorthodoxy*,[9] rather than admit that they themselves are drifting to the left of orthodoxy. The most dangerous part of this view is the drift. When one gives up the inerrancy of the Scriptures, how can he avoid giving up one by one the other major doctrines of the Christian faith? As one writer phrased it, "If neo-conservatism can maintain its view of an inerrantly-errant Bible without further departure from the remaining basic doctrines of the Christian faith, it will succeed in doing what no other group or institution has been able to do in American religious history."[10]

CHAPTER VII

THE CONSERVATIVE VIEW OF INSPIRATION

There are many misconceptions as to what the conservative view of inspiration really is. Some Liberals will launch a towering attack on a "mechanical" or "dictational" theory of inspiration and then will smugly sit back, thinking that they have demolished the conservative position, whereas in reality they have only demolished a straw man and have not even touched the conservative position. What, then, is the conservative view?

I. DEFINITION OF INSPIRATION

Although Conservatives have not been vague in defining the doctrine, their statements have often been ignored by the Liberals. Perhaps a series of definitions will clarify the conservative position. Charles Hodge has stated that "the common doctrine of the Church is, and ever has been, that inspiration was an influence of the Holy Spirit on the minds of certain select men, which rendered them the organs of God for the infallible communication of his mind and will."[1] In his classic work on the doctrine Benjamin B. Warfield gavè this definition: "Inspiration is . . . a supernatural influence exerted on the sacred writers by the Spirit of God, by virtue of which their writings are given Divine trustworthiness."[2] A modern commentator on Romans, Floyd E. Hamilton, defined it, "By inspiration we mean that the Holy Spirit of God so guided and controlled the writer of a book in the Old or New Testaments, that what he wrote was free from all errors of either fact or doctrine, and became the truth which God wanted his people to have."[3]

Conservatives make a definite point of identifying the Scriptures with the Word of God. When Ned B. Stonehouse discussed the unique features of the New Testament which distinguish it from all merely human writings, he stated, "Those who accept this high view of the New Testament, accordingly, do not shrink from identifying it as the Word of God, the infallible and inerrant rule of faith and life."[4] On the other hand, they will not identify inspiration with revelation. As Hodge phrased it, "The object of revelation is the communication of knowledge. The object or design of inspiration is to secure infallibility in teaching."[5] Neither will Conservatives confuse inspiration with insight, illumination, or human genius.

The word which is translated "inspired" (*theopneustos,* II Tim. 3:16) means "God-breathed." This obvious meaning continues to dominate Conservative thinking on the doctrine, for it is difficult not to associate the authoritative and the infallible with that which is "God-breathed." Loraine Boettner quoting Benjamin B. Warfield points out that "the very term in the Greek, *theopneustos,* means that a Divine product is breathed out by God."[6] The Greek word is unquestionably the strongest term that could have been used to convey the idea of divine origin and authority.

II. DENIAL OF DICTATION

Again and again Conservatives repudiate the theory of mechanical dictation. Griffith Thomas wrote, "Verbal inspiration does not mean mechanical dictation, as if the writers were only passive; dictation is not inspiration."[7] Hodge is just as emphatic, "The Church has never held what has been stigmatized as the mechanical theory of inspiration. The sacred writers were not machines. Their self-consciousness was not suspended; nor were their intellectual powers superseded. Holy men spake as they were moved by the Holy Ghost. It was men, not machines; not unconscious instruments, but living, thinking, willing minds, whom the Spirit used as his organs. Moreover, as inspiration did not involve the suspension or suppression of the human faculties, so neither did it interfere with the free exercise of the distinctive mental characteristics of the individual."[8]

B. F. Westcott speaks eloquently of the Bible as a unique Book combining the Divine and the human perfectly. "It is authoritative, for it is the voice of GOD; it is intelligible, for it is in the language of men."[9] In pursuing this thought farther, he says, "The language of the Lawgiver, the Historian, the Prophet, the Psalmist, the Apostle, is characteristic of the position which each severally occupied. Even when they speak most emphatically *the words of the Lord,* they speak still as men living among men; and the eternal truths which they declare receive the colouring of the minds through which they pass. . . . Everywhere there are traces of a personality not destroyed but even quickened by the action of the divine power, — of an individual consciousness not suspended but employed at every stage of the heavenly commission."[10]

Thus inspiration presupposes the supernatural providence of God by which these chosen men were prepared for the message that they would proclaim when the time came. God did not use just any man that happened to be alive, but rather He carefully trained and guided the ones who were to be His spokesmen. Edward J. Young has stated it this way, "Very wondrous was God's providential preparation and equipment of those men whom He had appointed to be the human instruments in the writing of the Scripture. Thus He prepared and raised up an Isaiah, a Jeremiah, a John, and a Paul. His work of providence and His special work of inspiration should be regarded as complementing one another."[11]

But at this point the Liberals are quick to charge that if man is thus active in inspiration, does this not mean that God's truth would be contaminated by man's sinfulness? Would not the truth have a large admixture of error?

III. DEFENSE OF INERRANCY

There is one reason, and one reason alone, that Conservatives hold so tenaciously to the inerrancy of Scripture: the Scripture itself teaches it. This is why John A. Witmer said, "If the verbal-plenary inspiration of the Bible and its concomitant inerrancy are the historic doctrine of the church and are commonly held today by the average Christian, these questions logically arise: Where did this belief come from? How did this doctrine develop? Why does it continue to persist under unrelenting attack? The only reasonable answer to these questions is, The Bible itself teaches it."[12] The Conservative will no more surrender this doctrine than he would the doctrine of the deity of Christ, justification by faith, or any other clearly taught Scriptural doctrine.

Inherent in this commitment to the Scriptural doctrine of inspiration is the conviction that the Lord Jesus Christ put His seal of approval and authentication on the Scriptures. As John Murray wrote, "The rejection of the inerrancy of Scripture means the rejection of Christ's own witness to Scripture. Finally and most profoundly, then, the very integrity of our Lord's witness is the crucial issue in this battle of the faith."[13] This does not mean that when the Lord mentioned Moses (Mark 7:10; 10:3, 5; 12:26, etc.), He was only defending the Mosaic authorship of the Pentateuch. On a much more crucial level, as H. C. G. Moule states, we must seek to determine "whether or no the Lord Jesus was altogether and in principle mistaken. He treated the Law, Prophets, and Psalms as a solid structure of historic fact and supernatural promise, divinely planned all through, divinely carried out and up from the foundation, and leading straight up to Himself. . . . If we revise the opinion of our Redeemer on this conspicuous point of His teaching, where shall we securely pause?"[14]

Once the words of the Lord Jesus Himself are set aside, there is no way to stop this side of bleak skepticism. This is not to say that faith would be impossible without an infallible Scripture, but it would be much more difficult. Samuel G. Craig has said, "Even if the Bible were only generally trustworthy, we could still have Christianity in a form sufficiently pure for men to be justified and sanctified and glorified. It should not be overlooked, however, that in that case we would not have a *Holy* Bible, because that which most makes the Bible a *Holy* Bible is its divine trustworthiness as contrasted with the uncertainty that characterizes all ordinary books. We expect of *Holy Scriptures* not only 'heavenliness of matter and efficacy of doctrine' but also 'infallible truth and divine authority.' Writings that lack such trustworthiness and authority may be highly esteemed but it is to sin against honest nomenclature to call them 'holy' writings."[15]

An analogy which may help to clarify the doctrine of inspiration is the parallel of the Incarnation. Just as the Lord Jesus Christ had two natures, the human and the divine, the written Word of God also has its human and divine sides. The union of the divine and the human did not make the human nature of Christ sinful or fallible, for Scripture expressly says that He "was in all points tempted like as we are, yet without sin" (Heb. 4:15). If the human nature of Christ is perfect, there is no inherent reason why the human element of the Bible could not be perfect as well. Admittedly the analogy is not perfect because it is between a Person and a thing, but at least it sheds light on the mystery of the human and divine elements in Scripture.

IV.   DEFENSE OF PERSPICUITY

Countless numbers of people who have been denied higher education read the Bible with understanding and benefit. This is what the Conservative means when he says that Scripture is "perspicuous," that is, it is capable of being understood by the average man without the explanations of either priests or theological scholars. "It is not denied that the Scriptures contain many things hard to be understood; that they require diligent study; that all men need the guidance of the Holy Spirit in order to [attain] right knowledge and true faith. But it is maintained that in all things necessary to salvation they are sufficiently plain to be understood even by the unlearned."[16] Since every man is personally responsible to God, God has graciously revealed His Word to help men meet their responsibility. God intended His Word for the average man, not just for the theologian.

V.   THE AUTOGRAPHA

The final court of appeal in all theological disputes must be to the text of the original Greek and Hebrew manuscripts. Conservatives are not contending for the infallibility of any translation, but only for the infallibility of the original documents. Undoubted Conservatives like James M. Gray have stated repeatedly that *"the record for whose inspiration we contend is the original record* — the autographs or parchments of Moses, David, Daniel, Matthew, Paul, or Peter, as the case may be, and not any particular translation or translations of them whatever. There is no translation absolutely without error, nor could there be, considering the infirmities of human copyists, unless God were pleased to perform a perpetual miracle to secure it."[17]

It is the sphere of textual criticism to detect and to remove as many of these copyist's errors as possible. The diligent labors of many scholars have brought the text of the Bible to an exceptionally high state of accuracy. In fact, one theologian has stated that "we possess the text of the Bible today in a form which is substantially identical with the autographs," and he is careful to state, "For theological study the appeal is to the most correct available text in the original language."[18]

VI. THE CANON

The word "canon" means basically "rule" or "standard." The word is applied by Protestants to the sixty-six Books of the Holy Bible. Conservatives maintain that these Books of the Old and New Testaments were canonical from the day that they were written. It may well have taken the people of God some time to recognize their canonicity, but the fact of inspiration assured their canonicity. Considering the ancient difficulty of transportation and communication, it is not surprising that time had to elapse before the community of faith came to realize the authority of each of these Books.

The Liberals wish to say that the Scriptural Books were regarded as ordinary books until centuries later when men "canonized" them in order to make them authoritative. In discussing the Old Testament canon, William Henry Green wrote, "The fundamental error which underlies all the arguments of the critics on this subject, and vitiates their conclusion, is the assumption that the books of the Old Testament were not written with the design of being held sacred and divinely authoritative; but in the course of time they came to be treated with a veneration which was not at first accorded to them."[19] This is why the Liberals will say that the Mosaic Pentateuch was "canonized" around 444 B.C. in the times of Ezra. In contrast to this, the Conservatives will say that every Book of the Bible was canonical at the time of its composition because it was inspired, but it may well have taken the redeemed community some time to recognize this.

Thus for the Conservative the Bible is both a human and a divine Book, but the human never distorts or corrupts the divine. Adolph Saphir stated it boldly, "I do not say that the Bible *contains* the Word of God. I say that the Bible *is* the Word of God. I think it is a most erroneous and dangerous thing to say that the Bible contains the Word of God. The Bible with its history, with its laws, with its poetry, with its maxims, with its biographies, with its epistles, with everything that is in it, is the Word of God." Yet he goes on to notice "the human element, the individuality of the men who wrote, the gradual growth, the progressive manifestations of Scripture."[20] With the psalmist the Conservative can say, "Thy testimonies have I taken as an heritage for ever: for they are the rejoicing of my heart" (Ps. 119:111).

PART III

THE ALLEGED ERRORS

CHAPTER VIII

THE ALLEGED ERRORS IN THE OLD TESTAMENT

At this point a definition of terms is in order. The Liberal will call anything in Scripture which he cannot explain an "error." This is a manifestation of his underlying assumption that Scripture is just another human book with all the human frailties and mistakes which an ordinary book has. Any classification of these errors usually includes textual errors (I Sam. 17:14-57; II Sam. 21:19); historical errors (Josh. 10:15, 43, 21); scientific errors such as the "primitive" world view of Genesis 1; errors in chronology or numbers (Gen. 5 and 11); and morally unworthy passages (I Sam. 15:33). Perhaps under the historical errors they would subsume "myths" or "legends," such as Jonah and the great fish. At least they would clearly deny the historicity of such accounts.

The Conservatives, on the other hand, will deny that any of these passages are errors. This is quite frankly a manifestation of his underlying assumption that Scripture is a uniquely inspired Book, and therefore perfectly trustworthy and infallible. Instead of calling these passages "errors," the Conservative would call them "problems" or "difficulties." Although the Conservative may not be able to account for some things in such passages, he will not automatically assume that there are "errors" in the Scripture. He would rather assume that his own understanding of the passages may be in error.

In a work of this size it is not possible to survey all of the alleged "errors" or "problems."[1] The best that can be done is a representative selection of the different kinds of passages which are often advanced by the Liberals as "errors." Although no attempt is made to list all possible explanations, enough have been given to show that even the most difficult passages do have good solutions to their problems. Most of these difficulties are simply illustrations of the flaws in the thinking of the critics; relatively few of them are actual problems in the text.

Genesis 1

Liberals like to refer to the first chapter of Genesis as "the majestic creation myth with which the Old Testament opens."[2] Because they refuse to accept the historical character of this passage, they can only treat it as mere fiction. It is granted that Genesis 1 does not intend to teach science, but it is in agreement with the evidence that science has uncovered. Peter W. Stoner has drawn up a list of some thirteen facts found in chronological order in Genesis 1, which are taught in modern scientific theories in the identical chronological order.[3] The chance that Moses could have guessed the correct order for thirteen facts Stoner estimates as one in 311,351,040.

But it is neither necessary nor desirable to effect a complete harmonization between Scripture and the current scientific theories, because the theories of men are continually changing. What is accepted at one time soon becomes out of date. As far as the origin of the universe is concerned, science will always be limited to speculative theories, because by the nature of the case the origin of the universe can never be observed or tested by men. In this instance the scientist must walk by faith as surely as the Christian believer. If one grants that there is a God and that He has revealed Himself in Scripture, this implies that Scripture is the only authentic account by the only Witness possible of events which can never again be observed. Certainly it is no less reasonable for a Christian to believe in Genesis 1 than it is for an unbeliever to "believe" in a soon-to-be-modified theory.

Genesis 3

This chapter also receives its share of derision as "the legend of the talking serpent." C. H. Dodd wrote bluntly, "Adam is a myth."[4] Sometimes the point is made that eating a fruit is too insignificant a thing to have such far reaching results. But this is the true nature of a valid test: it was not a great thing, but a small thing which was the basis of the test. It manifested all the more clearly the need for simple obedience in respecting God's right to one tree, which may well have looked very similar to the thousands of others from which they could eat. Such a test was eminently suitable for a free moral agent.

As far as the "talking serpent" is concerned, in a much later period of history God opened the mouth of Balaam's ass so that it could speak (Num. 22:28). A much more basic explanation, however, may be found in the presence of Satan. Theologians have long recognized the presence of the devil in the voice of the serpent. In fact, the New Testament identifies the devil and Satan as "that old serpent" (Rev. 12:9). This would indicate a variety of demonic possession which is also found in the New Testament (Mark 5:11-13).

But if the historicity of this account be rejected, how shall the origin of sin in the human soul be explained? If there were not a simple choice between the Divine Authority and the subtle lie, in what way could man come to moral maturity? There is nothing in the account that violated the sense of rectitude, or that is inconsistent with the primeval context in which it occurs. Without this passage the origin of sin in mankind would be an insoluble mystery.

GENESIS 5 AND 11

It is sometimes maintained that these two chapters do not give a sufficient time between Abraham and the flood and the flood and Adam in their chronologies. When the years of the ten generations are added together, there are only 1556 years from Adam to the birth of Shem; in the next ten generations there are only 492 years to the birth of Isaac. The claim is that this is insufficient time for these historical periods, but such a charge overlooks the purpose of these genealogies. They were not intended to supply chronological information, because the ancient world did not have the modern obsession with dates and time. A number of conservative theologians have pointed out that these are typically Hebrew genealogies.[5] By Hebrew custom they did not have to indicate father — son relationship. When the genealogy says that "Seth begat Enos," it may very well mean, "Seth begat [the father of] Enos," or even more remote descent. A good example of this is found in the typically Hebrew genealogy in Matthew 1:8. This is the contrast:

Old Testament history lists:	Matthew 1:8 gives:
Joram (II Kings 8:24.)	Joram begat
Ahaziah (II Kings 8:25.)	
Joash (II Kings 11:2.)	
Amaziah (II Kings 14:1.)	
Uzziah (II Chron. 26:1.)	Ozias (Uzziah).

In this case the genealogy means that Joram begat the great-grandfather of Uzziah. Another fact which makes it likely that there are gaps in this genealogy is that there are exactly ten generations between Adam and Noah, and ten generations between Noah and Abraham. This suggests that the genealogy was rounded off into easily remembered groups just as the genealogy in Matthew was shortened to make three groups of exactly fourteen each.

Thus all the statements of how many years old the patriarch was at the birth of his son are of the nature of incidental information. It was not designed to give exact chronological dating. God did not feel that the exact number of years that man had been on the earth was important enough to be divinely revealed in Scripture. Man's salvation is in no way dependent on that fact.

GENESIS 30:37-43

The charge is often made that modern genetic science has shown this passage to be abyssmal superstition. Jacob thought that whatever the flocks and herds looked at during copulation would be reflected in the color of their offspring. In the light of modern investigation this is nonsense. But there is no reason to expect Jacob to have modern scientific knowledge. He was doing the best he knew in the customs of his own day. The record says significantly that Jacob "set the faces of the flocks toward the ringstraked, and all the brown in the flock of Laban" (Gen. 30:40). This means that Jacob was also using ordinary methods of cross-breeding by putting the spotted flocks together with the white in order to secure more spotted offspring. Very probably Jacob did not know what method would be the most effective in securing his purpose, but he did the best he could and his attempts are accurately recorded. The context, however, clearly portrays Jacob's prosperity as the effect of God's providential care (Gen. 31:9). Some Conservatives feel that this is a simple miracle wrought in complete disregard of Jacob's planning.[6]

EXODUS 20:5; MATTHEW 5:45

It is a common complaint that the Old Testament portrait of the Lord as a "jealous God" is morally unworthy and inconsistent with the New Testament teaching of God as a loving Father. But it is an obvious fact that God sent the sun and rain on the just and the unjust in both Old and New Testament times, and just as surely God will not share His glory with another in any time. The Lord Jesus Himself taught clearly, "Ye cannot serve God and mammon" (Matt. 6:24). The apostle Paul cried out, "What agreement hath the temple of God with idols? for ye are the temple of the living God. . . . Wherefore come out from among them, and be ye separate, saith the Lord, and touch not the unclear thing; and I will receive you, and will be a Father unto you" (II Cor. 6:16-18). God is a Father only to those who have single-minded devotion to His will. This truth is found throughout the New Testament as well as the Old Testament, for James asks, "Know ye not that the friendship of the world is enmity with God? whosoever therefore will be a friend of the world is the enemy of God" (Jas. 4:4). For this reason Paul beseeches believers to present their bodies a "living sacrifice" to God (Rom. 12:1), and in a succeeding warning says, "For it is written, As I live, saith the Lord, every knee shall bow to me, and every tongue shall confess to God" (Rom. 14:11). Thus the New Testament portrays God as a "jealous" God just as the Old Testament does. He will never share a person's divided allegiance. Since God is man's highest Good, this in the only morally worthy attitude that God could assume.

NUMBERS 2:2-3; 11:16, 24-26; 12:4

When the Lord instructed the Israelites concerning their camping, the tabernacle was supposed to be in the midst of the camp (Num. 2:2-3), but later people are said to come out of the camp to get to the tabernacle (Num. 11:16, 24-26; 12:4). But there was supposed to be a considerable space between the tabernacle in the midst and the camp of the people "far off" round about the tabernacle (Num. 2:2). It would be just as true that the people would have to leave the camp proper to come to the place of the tabernacle in the center as it would be to go outside the camp area, "for the same language would be appropriately used of going out from any particular encampment to the open space in the centre where the sanctuary stood."[7] In addition to this it would be strange if, when Miriam was shut out of the camp for her leprosy, she should be closer to the tabernacle of the Lord than the Israelites who were within the camp (Num. 12:14). On another occasion when some Israelites went out to fight Amalekites and Canaanites, Scripture says plainly that the ark of the covenant of the Lord "departed not out of the camp" (Num. 14:44).

JOSHUA 10:15, 43, 21

In the conquest of the land of Canaan Joshua is said in one case to return to the camp at Gilgal (Josh. 10:15, 43), and in another he is said to return to Makkedah (Josh. 10:21). It may be, however, that verses 12-15 are a brief summary of the whole campaign from the book of Jasher.[8] The following verses describe the trapping of the five kings in the cave at Makkedah, the continuing pursuit of the enemy armies, the return to Makkedah to slay the five kings (vs. 21), the end of the campaign, and the final return to Gilgal (vs. 43). In this way Makkedah would be one camping stop on the way to Gilgal.

I SAMUEL 15:33

This is often thought of as one more example of the barbaric custom of human sacrifice to a divinity. This opinion, however, ignores the context, for the destruction of the Amalekites was a divine judgment pronounced upon them because of sin. Saul had not spared Agag from any compassion which he felt for him, but solely to have a royal trophy to exhibit before his throne. Because king Saul would not slay Agag, the old prophet Samuel had to perform the act. Samuel was not offering Agag as a sacrifice, but rather he was executing him as a condemned criminal, as Samuel's own words make clear (vs. 33). Scripture shows that many of these pagan tribes were unimaginably corrupt (Lev. 18:24-30). It was a merciful judgment of God that would not allow them to pollute the land any longer with their wickedness.

I SAMUEL 17:4-57; II SAMUEL 21:19

These two passages are sometimes cited as a contradiction. The Hebrew text does present a problem in this case. Whereas the account of David slaying the giant Goliath is extremely well known, very few people know that the Hebrew text of II Samuel 21:19 seems to state that Elhanan slew Goliath. The King James interprets the phrase by making it read that Elhanan "slew [the brother of] Goliath." It may be that this is after all the best interpretation because a parallel passage has that very reading in the Hebrew text (I Chron. 20:5). To the writers of these Old Testament Books these mighty deeds were so famous as to need no explanation; as the centuries passed, however, these brief references became liable to misinterpretation. There are some Conservatives who believe that this is an example of an early copyist's error which has obscured the text.[9]

I SAMUEL 28:6; I CHRONICLES 10:14

Some have thought that these two passages contradict one another. I Samuel says that Saul inquired of the Lord and did not get an answer, whereas I Chronicles says that Saul did not inquire of the Lord. The solution here is in the meaning of the two different Hebrew words which are used in the respective passages. I Samuel uses the word *Shaal*, which is the simple "He asked," with no thought of earnestness or of intended obedience. Saul was in the habit of asking for favors from God without rendering obedience. I Chronicles on the other hand uses the word *Darash*, which means "He sought for" or "searched after." Obviously Saul was not earnestly seeking the Lord with the intention of obeying His will. Thus a knowledge of Hebrew can sometimes completely remove a difficulty.

I SAMUEL 31:3-6; II SAMUEL 1:6-10

I Samuel claims that king Saul fell on his sword to slay himself, whereas II Samuel portrays an Amalekite as slaying Saul. A careful reading suggests at least two possible solutions to this difficulty. In the first place the account in II Samuel is that of an Amalekite who is obviously claiming to have slain Saul in order to get a reward from the succeeding king, David. The Amalekite may very well have lied, although David takes his admission at face value and orders him slain for having killed the Lord's anointed. On the other hand it may be that Saul failed to kill himself when he fell on his sword, and his armorbearer only thought that he had died (I Sam. 31:5). A few minutes later the Amalekite could have arrived to find Saul still alive, although wounded (II Sam. 1:9-10), and could have slain him. In either case a contradiction is not a necessary interpretation, but one that sometimes would occur to a superficial reader.

II SAMUEL 24:1; I CHRONICLES 21:1

In II Samuel God moved David to number Israel; in the other passage Satan provoked David to thus sin. But according to the Hebrew way of thinking (which is commonly accepted today) anything which God permitted was ascribed to Him. Thus Satan was the immediate tempter to provoke David to number the Israelites in unbelief. Satan, however, could not do this unless God permitted it; therefore God is the ultimately responsible Source. This leads back to the whole problem of the presence of Evil in the universe. In man's present state of understanding this problem is insoluble. The believer must simply trust that God knows that the end is worth the cost.

Psalm 18:40-44

This is another passage which is considered morally unworthy because David here speaks of crushing his enemies and treading them down as dirt in the streets. The Liberals often argue that the New Testament in a higher vein encourages love and well-doing for one's enemies (Matt. 5:43-44). There is no doubt that the New Testament does indeed present an advance on the teaching of the Old Testament. This Psalm, however, is strongly auto-biographical; David describes how the Lord has delivered him from his enemies and has avenged his persecution on them. Thus the poetic language which David uses to describe his triumphant attainment of the throne is not entirely out of place. In this case David's enemies were the enemies of the Theocracy, and it is fitting that the Lord should crush them and exalt David.

It is important to notice that both in the Old Testament and in the New Testament the Lord is portrayed as utterly destroying and crushing His enemies. It is part of the Divine Nature to hate evil. The Lord Jesus Christ pictures Himself as speaking in the judgment to the wicked, "Depart from me, ye cursed, into everlasting fire" (Matt. 25:41). The apostle Paul presents just as stern a scene when he describes the Lord's Second Coming "when the Lord Jesus shall be revealed from heaven with his mighty angels, in flaming fire taking vengeance on them that know not God, and that obey not the gospel of our Lord Jesus Christ; who shall be punished with everlasting destruction from the presence of the Lord, and from the glory of his power" (II Thes. 1:7-9). The writer to the Hebrews reminds his readers of the same thing, "It is a fearful thing to fall into the hands of the living God" (Heb. 10:31). The mawkish sentimentality that would excuse the crimes of sinners is foreign to the teaching of both the Old and New Testaments.

PROVERBS 26:4-5

"Answer not a fool according to his folly, lest thou also be like unto him. Answer a fool according to his folly, lest he be wise in his own conceit." This is a designed paradox, not a contradiction. These proverbs teach that one should not answer a fool according to his folly, lest one be considered a fool himself; on the other hand answer a fool according to his folly, lest the fool imagine himself wise. This kind of problem remains to the present day. A fool often cannot be silenced unless one uses foolish logic to refute him, and thus leaves himself open to the charge of folly. Just as surely the fool should be answered so that he would not get the impression that he is wise and his arguments unanswerable. Paradox is one of the more common methods of teaching which the Biblical writers use.

JONAH 1:17

One of the most repeated objections is "Jonah and the whale." This is not, however, an "error," for it is portrayed as a miracle. God "prepared" the great fish and distinctly preserved the prophet's life. Such objections are simply a manifestation of unbelief. The skeptic is philosophically committed to denying the supernatural; therefore, this passage cannot be true. For the one who believes in a Living God this passage is another example of God's providential care in seeing that His purpose will be accomplished through His messengers. When one admits the existence of a living and active God, there is nothing in the passage that is either incredible or unreasonable. Jonah was given the important commission of calling the great city of Nineveh to repentance, and God dealt with Jonah until he surrendered to the will of God and preached to the Ninevites.

CONCLUSION

A reverent study of the Old Testament will produce a firm conviction of its truth and trustworthiness. Certainly the prophets themselves manifested great fidelity and courage in recording messages which they felt were the Words of the Living God. "The distinguishing characteristic of the prophets, first of their speech and action and afterwards of their writings, was the firm and unwavering belief that they were instruments or organs of the Most

High, and that the thoughts which arose in their minds about Him and His Will, and the commands and exhortations which they issued in His Name, really came at His prompting, and were really invested with His authority."[10] The prophets did not use the Sophists' cleverness of speech; rather they spoke forth bluntly and faithfully their divine message. Some passages may indeed be difficult to interpret properly, but the interpreter should not therefore jump to the conclusion that there are errors in the text. There may be only failure in comprehension on the part of the interpreter.

It is always a wholesome thing for man to recognize his own limitations in thinking and understanding. A finite creature cannot hope to attain an infallible comprehension of a subject as vast as the Holy Scriptures. Apparently there never will be a correction of the warped and twisted thinking of the lost, but for the redeemed there is the hope of glorification when we shall know even as we are known. Until this glorious day comes, the believer must be content to understand in part and to walk in faith.

CHAPTER IX

THE ALLEGED ERRORS IN THE NEW TESTAMENT

Sometimes it is difficult to tell which alleged errors in the Bible are in vogue at the present moment. Biblical investigation, archaeological discoveries, or plain common sense often removes all questions of error from a Scriptural text. There are literally hundreds of Scripture passages which were once cited as "errors" which now are not mentioned by Liberal critics because the point at issue has proved to be an outstanding example of the trust-worthiness of Scripture.

Throughout most of the nineteenth century, one of these passages, Acts 14:6, was presented as a flagrant example of the historical inaccuracy of "whoever wrote Acts." The argument was that the writer of Acts mentioned Paul's flight to Lystra and Derbe as though he was just entering the province of Lycaonia, whereas Iconium, which he had just left, was also known to be a part of Lycaonia. But this was one of the passages which Sir William Ramsay checked for the historical accuracy of Acts. His archaeological investigations showed that Iconium was made a part of Phrygia only during A.D. 37-72; both before and after this time it was a part of Lycaonia. Thus the one period in history in which Luke's statement could be true was the very period in which the apostle had indeed fled to Lystra and Derbe, "cities of Lycaonia." Thus at one stroke this passage transformed Sir William Ramsay's opinion of the authenticity of the Book of Acts, and at the same time was permanently removed from the list of "errors."[1]

In the remainder of this chapter let us consider a necessarily selective list of representative passages from the New Testament recently cited as "difficulties" or "errors." At the present time these are "live" issues in some areas, although I am aware that many of these passages may soon be removed from any further list of "errors."

MATTHEW 1:1-17; LUKE 3:23-38

The two genealogies of Christ are often thought to be mutually contradictory. The Liberals are quick to point out that between Joseph and David there are only two names which are similar. But by common consent Matthew's Gospel is intended for the Jewish reader and portrays the Lord Jesus Christ as the rightful King of the Jews. Logically, therefore, Matthew presents the royal genealogy through the kingly line to David, and on to Abraham. Although Matthew makes clear that Joseph was not the father of the Lord Jesus (1:18-25), Joseph was the husband of Mary, and thus the full legal title to the Davidic throne passed from Joseph to the Lord Jesus. Because God's curse fell on king Jechonia (Coniah) and his descendents, the Lord Jesus could not have actual physical descent from him (Jer. 22:24-30).

In contrast the Gospel of Luke is intended for Gentile readers and presents Christ as the Universal Man. Mary dominates the first chapters of Luke, and hence it is probable that the genealogy is hers. But it would not be customary to name a woman in a Jewish genealogy. Joseph, therefore, is listed as related to Heli; probably Joseph was his son-in-law. The word "son" is not in the Greek text in these verses; in each case it is a genitive of relationship. The relationship can be that between son-in-law and father-in-law just as easily as it could be son to father. Some writers make a considerable point of the Davidic descent of Mary.[2] Certainly in the controversies with Christians the Jews would have discredited the Messianic claim of Christ if Mary had not been of Davidic descent, but no Jew ever attempted to deny the Davidic lineage of the Lord Jesus. There are other possible explanations for these genealogies, but the majority of conservative scholars seems to favor this one (Bengel, 'Lightfoot, Alexander, Godet, Broadus, A. T. Robertson, and others).[3]

MATTHEW 5:33-37

The charge is sometimes made that Christ is here contradicting the Old Testament law. But the language which our Lord quotes is drawn from rabbinical interpretation of the Old Testament. Part of the language is based on Deuteronomy 23:21-23, which deals with the fulfillment of vows, and part is based on Leviticus 19:12, which deals with swearing falsely. Because the Jews were given to uttering innumerable minor oaths, the Lord is here showing the danger of using that which is holy to dignify frivolous occasions or subjects. Broadus states that the Jews were known to swear in ordinary conversation by the temple, the dishes in it, the altar, the lamb, the law, Moses, the prophets, the life of the rabbis, and a host of other things.[4]

It is this frivolous use of minor oaths which the Lord is attacking, and not the use of a formal oath on solemn or legal occasions. In His trial before the high priest, the Lord Jesus allowed Himself to be put under oath by the high priest, and He did answer under oath (Matt. 26:63-64). Obviously the Lord did not mean to outlaw all legal oaths, any more than He intended to outlaw capital punishment by His words on killing (Matt. 5:21-22). When in a train of solemn thought, the apostle Paul also sometimes called God as his witness (Rom. 1:9; 12:1).

MATTHEW 17:27

Some of these alleged "errors" are simply miracles. The account of Christ telling Peter to find the coin in the mouth of the fish is one example of this. Skeptics seem to attack this solely because of antisupernatural bias. Typical of such naturalistic bias is Plummer's explanation that Peter sold the fish and thus received money "from" the fish.[5] The answer to all such objections is in the Person of the Lord Jesus Christ. If He is indeed the Divine Son of God in human flesh, it is reasonable to expect miracles in His ministry. One who believes in the miracles of the Incarnation and the bodily Resurrection of Christ should have no trouble believing in lesser miracles connected with our Lord. If one rejects these great miracles connected with the Person of the Lord, there is no Scriptural reason for calling him a Christian. Thus the finding of the coin is not an "error" at all, but rather an act of the Son of God.

MATTHEW 27:3-10; ACTS 1:16-19

These two accounts of the events connected with the death of Judas the betrayer are often regarded as contradictions, but it is possible to harmonize them. One probable explanation is this order of events:

1. Judas hurled the 30 tetradrachms to the priests in the temple. Matt. 27:3.
2. He then went out and hanged himself. Matt. 27:5.

3. Either the rope or the branch broke; he fell upon a rock and received mortal wounds. Acts 1:18.
4. This bloody act was regarded as polluting the field. Acts 1:19.
5. The priests later used the 30 tetradrachms to buy the field to bury aliens in. Matt. 27:7.

A notorious suicide is often regarded as too well known to require detailed explanations, and differing details should not be regarded as contradictory unless the facts cannot be reconciled.

MATTHEW 27:37; MARK 15:26; LUKE 23:38; JOHN 19:19

Although each of the four Gospel writers record the inscription on the cross, none of them give it with the same words. But the writers were not under obligation to quote all the inscription. Perhaps the full inscription read, "This is Jesus of Nazareth, the King of the Jews." Each Evangelist then quoted part of the inscription. But we must also remember that the inscription was written in three different languages, Latin, Greek, and Hebrew. The variations may well have been original in the different languages; one Evangelist quoting from one language, and another translating from another. There is certainly no necessity of assuming that slight variations must be irreconcilable contradictions.

MARK 6:34-44; MARK 8:1-9

Some Liberals will say that the feeding of the four thousand in Mark 8 is just a repetition of the feeding of the five thousand (Mark 6), because Mark did not realize that they were the same event. Although the circumstances and the context are clearly different, some Liberals hold that these two accounts are inaccurate descriptions of the same miracle. The only reason for this position is apparently that one such miracle is easier to believe than two. But if one grants that the Lord Jesus Christ did indeed perform the miracle of the feeding of the five thousand, there is no inherent difficulty in His feeding on a different occasion four thousand others. Scripture records that the Lord Jesus healed many blind men and cleansed many lepers (Mark 1:32-34; 3:10-12; 6:56); surely some of His miracles of sustenance were repeated as well.

MARK 14:30, 68, 72; MATTHEW 26:34, 74-75; LUKE 22:34, 60-61

Another alleged contradiction is Mark's phrasing of Jesus' words to Peter, "Before the cock crow twice, thou shalt deny me thrice," whereas Matthew and Luke do not mention the cock's crowing twice. But this is actually a case of general information and more detailed information. Matthew and Luke present the general fact that Peter denied the Lord Jesus before the cock crew. Mark, however, was the disciple of Peter and by tradition took down the very words of Peter. Surely Peter could never forget the exact words which the Lord addressed to him on that dreadful occasion; thus he tells the more detailed account that the cock actually crowed twice while Peter was denying his Lord. It is to be expected that one who was present on a certain occasion will be able to recall details which others who give a general account will omit. Mark simply recorded in detail what Peter had told him about the Lord's Passion. This is one more evidence for the independent testimony of the four evangelists concerning the life of the Lord Jesus Christ.

LUKE 16:1-13

There are a host of contradictory interpretations on the parable of the Unjust Steward. Any interpretation, however, that reflects on the moral suitability of commending the Unjust Steward is based on sheer misunderstanding of the parable. The lord who commends the unjust steward (vs. 8) is certainly the master of the steward, and not the Lord Jesus. The Lord related this parable to drive home one truth, that if an unjust person exercises forethought and prudence (not to mention shrewdness!) in order to attain his personal advantage in this world, how much more should the believer exercise similar diligence and planning in order to attain the heavenly glory to which he is called? It is clear that the Lord is not commending to our attention the dishonesty of the steward, because He speaks strongly about faithfulness which the believer is expected to manifest in small things as well as large (vs. 10-12). But the believer should make his present opportunities count for the world to come. Diligence and forethought are valuable in the spiritual realm as well as in the material.

ACTS 7:4; GENESIS 11:26, 32; 12:4

One of the difficulties in Stephen's sermon is his mention of

Abraham's departure from the land of Haran after his father was dead. Genesis tells us that Terah lived seventy years and begat Abram, Nahor, and Haran, that Terah died in Haran at the age of two hundred five years, and that Abram departed out of Haran at the age of seventy-five years. This does sound as though Abraham departed while Terah still had sixty years to live. What, then, does Stephen's statement mean? Many explanations have been advanced. It may be that Abraham was the youngest son in Genesis 11:26 and that he was born sixty years after Haran. It is also possible that Stephen is referring to Terah's spiritual death in idolatry. The fact that Philo agrees with Stephen on this point may imply that there was a Septuagint text which had this reading, but is no longer extant.[7] It may be that we do not have enough historical evidence to solve this problem. This does not mean that there is an "error" here, but that the information available to the present generation is incomplete. It is not incumbent on the expositor to "prove" each interpretation correct; it is only necessary to show that explanations exist. Faith will rest in confidence on ultimate understanding (I Cor. 13:12). Man's present understanding is imperfect, and hasty judgments are always suspect. So much of Scripture that was once thought to be insolubly difficult has since been clarified that the believer can well wait in patience for this difficulty to be resolved also.

ACTS 7:15-16; GENESIS 23:16-18

Stephen related that Abraham bought a sepulchre from the sons of Emmor (or Hamor), but the Old Testament described Jacob as doing this (Gen. 33:19). Abraham did build an altar at Shechem, and no doubt he purchased the land on which to build it. In later years, as Knowling suggests, Jacob may again have purchased this land.[8] On the other hand, Stephen may be telescoping the two accounts.[9] Apparently neither Stephen nor the hostile audience felt that there was a difficulty or contradiction involved. Again it may be that both Stephen and his hostile judges had more information than the modern scholars have available.

ACTS 9:7; 22:9

The Liberals cite these two passages as an obvious example of a contradiction. Acts 9:7 states that the men with Paul on the Damascus road heard a voice, and in 22:9 it says that they did not

hear the voice. This is clearly regarded by the Liberals as an
insoluble contradiction.[10] However, the natural interpretation of
these two passages is that, just as the men with Paul saw the light,
but did not see the Person of the Lord, so they heard the sound of
His voice without understanding the words which He uttered. Because Luke knew the truth of this occurrence, he does not seek a
mechanical agreement, but rather uses his narrative phraseology
freely.

There is also a technical grammatical explanation in the nature
of the Greek cases. The accusative case in Greek is normally the
case of content; it explains "what." On the other hand, the genitive
case is usually the case that specifies or describes. The verb "I
hear" may take either the accusative or the genitive case after it
as direct object. When the accusative case occurs after "I hear,"
it refers to the content of what is heard, that is, the words. On the
day of Pentecost Peter addressed his audience, "Men, Israelites,
hear ye these words [akousate tous logous]" (Acts 2:22). This
construction is also found in Acts 4:4; 5:5, 11, 24; 7:12, 54; 8:6; 9:4;
10:22, 33, 44; 11:18; 13:7, 44; 15:7, and regularly throughout the
Book. When the genitive case follows "I hear," it usually specifies
one person rather than another or one thing rather than another.
In Acts there are numerous examples of this genitive after "I hear,"
for example, in Acts 3:22-23 the people must hear "that prophet"
and not another (tou prophetou ekeinou); again in 4:19 the
apostles question hearing "you" rather than God; in 6:11, 14 they
hear "him," Stephen, and not another; in 7:34 God heard their
"groaning," not their rejoicing, and many other instances throughout
Acts. These uses are not without exception, but they are usual.

In Acts 9:7 the men heard a "voice" in the genitive case; this
specifies a voice rather than a thunderclap, or some other sound.
In 22:9 the men did not hear the voice in the accusative case;
that is, they did not hear the content of the voice, namely the
words uttered. A parallel to this is found in Acts 17:32 in which
the Athenians "heard the resurrection" (accusative); that is, the
content, the doctrine of the resurrection. Some of the group then
said, "We will hear thee (genitive) again," specifying Paul without
referring to content. They had heard enough about that doctrine.
Thus the grammatical explanation simply confirms the logical one.[11]
Here again the attitude of unbelief looks for the contradictions; the
attitude of faith seeks the harmony of Scripture.

It is significant that so distinguished a grammatical authority as Nigel Turner denies that there are any exceptions in the New Testament to this grammatical rule, and carefully shows that each of the so-called exceptions can have an explanation in the strictest grammatical meaning of the cases used.[12]

ROMANS 3:28; 4:5; JAMES 2:14-26

Paul's doctrine of salvation by faith and James' doctrine of the necessity of works have often been advanced as contradictions. A number of Liberals have held that James "shows no comprehension of Paul's doctrine of salvation through faith."[13] But James is by no means ignorant of the doctrine of faith (Jas. 1:3-6; 2:1); what he is attacking is a dead "faith" which cannot transform the life. He urges being a doer of the Word and not just a hearer (Jas. 1:22), and he scorns an empty profession which cannot act (Jas. 2:14-16). Just as a body without the spirit is not a living body, so faith without works is not a "living" faith (Jas. 2:26). The error that James was attacking has been a deep-seated and pernicious one. In all ages of the church there have been people who have professed to be Christian, but whose lives have denied the faith.

On the other hand, the apostle Paul was far from saying that the kind of life one lived did not matter as long as he was a believer. After insisting that man is saved through faith alone, Paul goes on to present a thorough doctrine of the Christian life which follows salvation (Rom. 12:1-21). The believer is to present his body a living sacrifice to God (vss. 1-2), to manifest brotherly love (vs. 10), to continue in prayer (vs. 12), to manifest hospitality (vs. 13), to do good to one's enemies (vs. 20), and to overcome evil with good (vs. 21). Again and again he stresses that the believer should "maintain good works" (Tit. 3:8, 14). Thus Paul teaches that a genuine faith alone will save and will transform the life; James teaches that a false faith which does not change the life cannot save.

I CORINTHIANS 7:20-22

Some have thought that it was morally unworthy for Paul to advise slaves to remain as slaves and not to speak out against such a horrible institution as slavery. But Paul knew that the ethics which he was advocating (Phil. 2:3-8) would ultimately destroy the institution of slavery. On the other hand, to attempt to overthrow the social and political order would simply lead to anarchy, and thus Paul urges all Christians to obey the civil rulers (Rom. 13). The Scriptures do not portray the world as getting better and better through the ministry of the church; rather the world will apparently deteriorate morally and spiritually (I Tim. 4:1; II Tim. 3:1-13). Many times well-meaning believers have become champions of social reform, only to find that they must leave the world just about as they found it. The most effective social reform is the one which the apostle Paul practiced: the simple proclamation of the Gospel. When men's hearts are renewed by the grace of God, their influence in society is spontaneously directed toward the good. Many times converted men can succeed in acting together to reform abuses, but apart from the transforming power of the new birth, the preacher has little hope of changing social and political institutions which are dominated by unsaved men.

I CORINTHIANS 10:8; NUMBERS 25:9

Paul cites an Old Testament example of God's judgment on sin in which 23,000 people fell on one day. The Old Testament record says that 24,000 people died in the plague. If read carefully, this is not a contradiction because Paul is giving the deaths "in one day," whereas the Old Testament account gives the total deaths "in the plague." All the people did not necessarily die on the same day, even though most of them did. Paying attention to the exact words in Scripture often will remove such apparent contradictions.

JUDE 14, 15

When Jude refers to the patriarch Enoch, he seems to quote directly from the apocryphal book of Enoch. Liberals hold that Jude thought he was quoting from the writings of the ancient patriarch, whereas in reality he was quoting a non-inspired book which had no connection with the real patriarch. But if, as conservatives traditionally hold, God revealed to Moses those facts concerning Enoch which appear in Genesis, there is no inherent reason that He could not reveal more concerning Enoch, either then or in later years, which was not recorded in Scripture. There could be an authentic tradition embodying Enoch's teaching which was later incorporated into the apocryphal book of Enoch. All that the conservative must hold is that the actual words which Jude quoted were true and authentic, not that the whole apocryphal book be true.

New Testament writers often quote from non-inspired writings (Acts 17:28; I Cor. 15:33; Tit. 1:12). All that is demanded is that the statement quoted be true. Paul did not say that the writings of Aratus or Menander were inspired, but individual statements which were true and which fit Paul's line of thought he would quote. The only difference in the case of Jude is that to be true the statement must be the authentic words of Enoch, which are not elsewhere cited in Scripture. This practice of citing an authentic tradition not found in the Old Testament occurs in a number of New Testament passages: Paul stated that Saul reigned for 40 years (Acts 13:21); he named the magicians who withstood Moses before Pharaoh (II Tim. 3:8); these facts are not recorded in the Old Testament. This does not mean that these are inventions; it means that these New Testament writers were citing accurate traditions which have not survived outside of the New Testament references.

REVELATION 1:4-5

Some of the 19th century grammarians used to point out at great length the many grammatical "errors" in the New Testament, especially in the Book of Revelation. Although the discoveries of the papyri have shown the New Testament to be written in the every day language of the first century, this charge of grammatical "errors" is still found in some works. Funk's translation of the Blass – Debrunner Grammar mentioned that the grammar in Rev. 1:4 "jarred upon every cultured ear."[14] These grammarians seem to think that the New Testament would have had to be written in the style of Thucydides or Herodotus in order to be "correct." This is as naive as to say that a good English writer should write like Shakespeare! The modern writer who tried this affected style would be pitied (or perhaps ignored) rather than admired. The whole question of style is a subjective one, for often what one critic condemns as an "error" another will commend.

In Revelation 1:4 the phrase "the one who is and who was and who is coming" follows a preposition (apo) which normally requires the genitive case, but here the phrase is in the nominative case. The Greek of the first century often put a name in the nominative case regardless of other grammatical relations. This practice was so common that some modern grammarians call this usage the "nominative of appellation."[15] This great divine name is put in the nominative case as a form of striking emphasis. No thoughtful reader would misunderstand the Biblical writer. The same grammatical explanation fits in Revelation 1:5 in which the nominative case name, "the Faithful Witness," is in apposition to "Jesus Christ," in the genitive case. Again a name takes precedence over other grammatical relationships.

Conservatives do not teach that the Holy Spirit gave all writers of Scripture a grammatically "perfect" style; rather the Holy Spirit used the individual writer's own style and his own vocabulary to communicate the divine revelation intended. One need not expect fishermen like John and Peter to manifest the same grammatical precision that a theologian like Paul or a physician like Luke would naturally use. In the emotional stress of the great apocalyptic vision which John received in Revelation it is not surprising if the grammar becomes strained in John's attempt to record what was overwhelming his soul (Rev. 1:17).

CONCLUSION

This list of representative passages is enough to illustrate that there are explanations for difficulties in Scripture. It is not logically necessary to prove a precise interpretation for each passage; it is only necessary to show that solutions exist. The reader is then impelled to face again the question of whether he will believe the divine Word of the Living God revealed in the Holy Scriptures. The skeptic can always multiply objections, but the believer may rest on the trustworthiness of the revelation which he has found sufficient to cleanse his heart and to transform his life.

If the reader is one who does not know the Lord Jesus Christ as his personal Saviour from sin, will he now turn to God in faith and seek in the Bible the passages which can give him eternal life? (John 3:36; 3:16; Rom. 6:23; 10:13). "Believe on the Lord Jesus Christ, and thou shalt be saved." The difficulties evaporate before the warmth of the love of God.

Alfred Cave has well said, "The Bible is a book for man as man. It is neither a treatise of theology, nor a manual of science; a handbook of law, nor a collection of sermons. Sermons are for an age; a law code would soon need lawyers for its interpretation; theology is for the theologian; science is for the scientist. But the Bible is not the book of an age or of a class. It appeals to all, and like the greatest of whom the Bible speaks, the common people hear it gladly."[16]

When we consider the real grandeur of the Bible and the power of its influence through the ages, the quibbling "errors" which skeptics hope to prove in it pale into insignificance. As Frederick W. Robertson has written,

> This collection of books has been to the world what no other book has ever been to a nation. States have been founded on its principles. Kings rule by a compact based on it. Men hold the Bible in their hands when they prepare to give solemn evidence affecting life, death, or property. . . . Men who know nothing of the architecture of a Christian cathedral, can yet tell you all about the pattern of the holy temple. Even this shows us the influence of the Bible. The orator holds a thousand men for half an hour breathless — a thousand men as one, listening to his single word. But this word of God has held a thousand nations for thrice a thousand years spellbound; held them by an abiding power, even the universality of its truth; and we feel it to be no more a collection of books, but *the* book."[17]

NOTES

CHAPTER II:
THE NEW TESTAMENT TEACHING ON INSPIRATION

[1]Original translation from the Greek by the author.

[2]The verb may be either an indicative or an imperative; the imperative is chosen by Chrysostom, Augustine, Luther, Calvin, Keil, etc.; the indicative by Westcott, Godet, etc.

[3]Newport White, *The Expositor's Greek Testament*, Vol. IV, p. 175.

CHAPTER III: THE HISTORIC FAITH OF THE CHURCH

[1]*I Clement*, XLV, 2, 3.

[2]IV, 2, 3.

[3]III, 1, 1.

[4]*Epistolae*, 82, i, 3.

[5]B. F. Westcott, *An Introduction to the Study of the Gospels*, Appendix B, pp. 413-452.

[6]St. Louis edition of Luther's works, III, 21.

[7]Luther's works, XV, 1481.

[8]Calvin, *Institutes*, book IV, 8, 9.

[9]Calvin, book IV, 8, 6.

[10]Calvin, book I, 7, 4.

[11]John Wesley, "Preface," *Sermons* (3rd American ed.), I, 6.

[12]Wesley, *Journal*, VI, 117.

[13]Philip Hughes, *Theology of the English Reformers*.

[14]Luther's *Small Catechism*, p. 41.

[15]J. Macpherson, *The Westminster Confession of Faith*, p. 35.

[16]Macpherson, p. 35.

[17]Macpherson, p. 36.

[18]T. E. Engelder, *Scripture Cannot Be Broken*, p. 30.

[19]Edward J. Young, *Thy Word Is Truth*, p. 184.

[20]"Bible," *The Encyclopedia of Christianity*, (General editor, Edwin Palmer) Vol. I, p. 659.

CHAPTER IV: THE LIBERAL VIEW OF INSPIRATION

[1]Schleiermacher, *The Christian Faith*, p. 593.

[2]H. E. Fosdick, *The Modern Use of the Bible*, p. 30.

[3]Fosdick, pp. 163-164.

[4]Henry P. Van Dusen, *The Vindication of Liberal Theology*, p. 32.

[5]Van Dusen, p. 115.

[6]Rudolf Bultmann, *Jesus Christ and Mythology*, pp. 16-17.

[7]Reinhold Niebuhr, *Reflections on the End of an Era*, p. 48.

[8]Daniel D. Williams, "Niebuhr and Liberalism" in *Reinhold Niebuhr, His Religious, Social, and Political Thought*, edited by Kegley and Bretall, p. 194.

[9]L. Harold DeWolf, *The Case for Theology in Liberal Perspective*, p. 43.
[10]DeWolf, *A Theology of the Living Church*, pp. 72-73.
[11]Paul Tillich, "The Word of God" in Anshen, *Language: An Enquiry into its Meaning and Function*, pp. 122-123.
[12]Tillich, pp. 125-126.
[13]Emil Brunner, *Revelation and Reason*, p. 9, note 13.

CHAPTER V:
THE NEO-ORTHODOX VIEW OF INSPIRATION

[1]Karl Barth, *Church Dogmatics*, Vol. I, Part 2, p. 507.
[2]Barth, I, 2, p. 512.
[3]Barth, I, 2, p. 507.
[4]Barth, I, 2, p. 510.
[5]Barth, I, 2, pp. 528-529.
[6]Emil Brunner, *The Theology of Crisis*, p. 41.
[7]Brunner, *Religionsphilosophie*, pp. 77-78.
[8]Brunner, *Dogmatics*, I, 47.
[9]Charles Harold Dodd, *The Authority of the Bible*, p. 233.
[10]Brunner, *Dogmatics*, I, 49.
[11]C. H. Dodd, *Epistle of Paul to the Romans*, xxxv.
[12]Dodd, *Romans*, p. 79.
[13]Barth, *Romans*, p. 171.
[14]Barth, *Church Dogmatics*, III, 3, pp. 522-523. He does believe that "nothingness" is a powerful influence.
[15]Barth, *Dogmatics*, III, 3, 531.
[16]Gustaf Wingren, *Theology in Conflict*, p. 125.
[17]Barth, *Dogmatics*, I, 2, 530.
[18]William Hordern, *The Case for a New Reformation Theology*, p. 59.
[19]P. T. Forsyth quoted in Gwilym Griffith, *The Theology of P. T. Forsyth*, p. 97.

CHAPTER VI:
THE NEO-EVANGELICAL VIEW OF INSPIRATION

[1]E. J. Carnell, *The Case for Orthodox Theology*, p. 111.
[2]L. H. DeWolf, A review of *The Case for Orthodox Theology* in *Journal of Bible and Religion*, October, 1959.
[3]Daniel Stevick, *Beyond Fundamentalism*, p. 95.
[4]Stevick, p. 108.
[5]B. Ramm, *Special Revelation and the Word of God*, p. 64.
[6]Carnell, p. 128.
[7]Carnell, p. 123.
[8]B. Ramm, *The Christian View of Science and Scripture*, p. 29.
[9]Ramm, p. 29.
[10]Harold Lindsell, "Is the Bible Wholly Reliable?" *Christian Life*, XXVII, 1, 56, May, 1965.

CHAPTER VII:
THE CONSERVATIVE VIEW OF INSPIRATION

[1]Charles Hodge, *Systematic Theology*, vol. I, p. 154.
[2]Benjamin B. Warfield, *The Inspiration and Authority of the Bible*, p. 131.
[3]Floyd E. Hamilton, *The Epistle to the Romans*, pp. 11-12.
[4]Ned B. Stonehouse, (ed.), *The Infallible Word*, p. 90.
[5]Hodge, *Systematic Theology*, vol. I, p. 155.
[6]Loraine Boettner, *Studies in Theology*, p. 21.
[7]W. H. Griffith Thomas, "Inspiration," *Bibliotheca Sacra*, CXVIII, 469 (January—March, 1961), p. 43.
[8]Hodge, *Systematic Theology*, vol. I, p. 157.
[9]Brooke Foss Westcott, *An Introduction to the Study of the Gospels*, p. 8.
[10]B. F. Westcott, *An Introduction*, p. 13.
[11]Edward J. Young, *Thy Word Is Truth*, p. 70.
[12]John A. Witmer, "The Biblical Evidence for the Verbal-Plenary Inspiration of the Bible," *Bibliotheca Sacra*, CXXI, 483 (July—September, 1964), p. 244.
[13]John Murray, "The Attestation of Scripture," in *The Infallible Word*, edited by N. B. Stonehouse and Paul Woolley, p. 40.
[14]Handley C. G. Moule, *To My Younger Brethren*, p. 57.
[15]Samuel G. Craig, "The Testimony of the Scriptures to their own Trustworthiness," *Princeton Theological Review*, XXII, 2 (April, 1924), p. 306-307.
[16]Hodge, *Systematic Theology*, vol. I, pp. 183 184,
[17]James M. Gray, "The Inspiration of the Bible," *The Fundamentals For Today*, ed. Charles L. Feinberg, p. 127.
[18]Johannes G. Vos, "Bible," *The Encyclopedia of Christianity*, General Editor, Edwin H. Palmer, I, p. 659.
[19]William Henry Green, *General Introduction to the Old Testament, The Canon*, p. 26.
[20]Adolph Saphir, *The Divine Unity of Scripture*, p. 37.

CHAPTER VIII:
THE ALLEGED ERRORS IN THE OLD TESTAMENT

[1]For a more extensive treatment see John W. Haley, *The Alleged Discrepancies of the Bible;* George W. DeHoff, *Alleged Bible Contradictions Explained.*
[2]Georgia Harkness, *The Faith by which the Church Lives*, p. 140.
[3]Peter W. Stoner, *Science Speaks*, pp. 11-33.
[4]C. H. Dodd, *Epistle of Paul to the Romans*, p. 79.
[5]Benjamin B. Warfield, *Biblical and Theological Studies*, pp. 242-244.
[6]*The New Scofield Reference Bible*, p. 44.
[7]James Orr, *The Problem of the Old Testament*, p. 168.
[8]John W. Haley, *The Alleged Discrepancies of the Bible*, p. 374.
[9]See Gleason L. Archer, Jr., *A Survey of the Old Testament Introduction*, p. 274.
[10]William Sanday, *Inspiration*, p. 394.

CHAPTER IX:
THE ALLEGED ERRORS IN THE NEW TESTAMENT

[1]W. M. Ramsay, *St. Paul the Traveler and the Roman Citizen*, pp. 110 ff.; *The Bearing of Recent Discovery on the Trustworthiness of the N.T.*, pp. 35 ff.

[2]N. Geldenhuys, *Luke*, p. 152.

[3]See the different views listed in A. T. Robertson, *Harmony of the Gospels*, pp. 259-262.

[4]Broadus, *Matthew*, p. 114.

[5]Plummer, *Matthew*, p. 247.

[6]Plummer, *Luke*, p. 380.

[7]F. F. Bruce, *Acts*, Grand Rapids, 1954, pp. 146-147, note 31.

[8]Knowling, *Acts* in the *Expositor's Greek Testament*, vol. 2, p. 185.

[9]F. F. Bruce, *Acts*, p. 149, note 39.

[10]L. Harold DeWolf, *A Theology of the Living Church*, p. 69.

[11]For further grammatical discussion see A. T. Robertson, *Word Pictures*, vol. III, pp. 117-118; J. H. Moulton, *Grammar of New Testament Greek*, vol. I, "Prolegomena," p. 66.

[12]For an interesting treatment of these examples see Turner's *Grammatical Insights into the New Testament*, pp. 87-90.

[13]Morton Scott Enslin, *The Literature of the Christian Movement*, p. 330.

[14]*Greek Grammar*, p. 75.

[15]Dana and Mantey, *Manual Grammar of the Greek New Testament*, p. 69.

[16]A. Cave, *The Inspiration of the Old Testament*, p. 494.

[17]F. W. Robertson, A Sermon on Inspiration, *Sermons*, pp. 828-829.

A SELECT BIBLIOGRAPHY

A. Important Articles

Andersen, Francis I. "We speak . . . in the Words . . . which the Holy Ghost teacheth," *Westminster Theological Journal*, XXII (May, 1960), 113-132.

Craig, Samuel G. "The Testimony of the Scriptures to Their Own Trustworthiness," *Princeton Theological Review*, XXII (April, 1924), 303-325.

Gray, James M. "The Inspiration of the Bible." In *The Fundamentals for Today*, ed. Charles L. Feinberg. Grand Rapids: Kregel Publications, 1958, pp. 125-145.

Hughes, Philip E. "The Knowledge of God: The Inspiration of the Bible." In *Basic Christian Doctrines*, ed. C. F. H. Henry. New York: Holt, Rinehart and Winston, 1962, pp. 14-20.

Lindsell, Harold. "A Historian Looks at Inerrancy," *Bulletin of the Evangelical Theological Society*, VIII (1965), 3-12.

Munhall, L. W. "Inspiration." In *The Fundamentals for Today*, ed. Charles L. Feinberg. Grand Rapids: Kregel Publications, 1958, pp. 147-158.

Pinnock, Clark H. "A Defense of Biblical Infallibility." Philadelphia: Presbyterian and Reformed Publishing Company, 1967, 32 pp.
          "Our Source of Authority: the Bible," *Bibliotheca Sacra*, CXXIV, 494 (April-June, 1967), 150-156.

Preus, Robert D. "The Nature of the Bible." In *Christian Faith and Modern Theology*, ed. C. F. H. Henry. New York: Channel Press, 1964.

Ryrie, Charles C. "The Importance of Inerrancy," *Bibliotheca Sacra*, CXX, 478 (April-June, 1963), 137-144.

Thomas, W. H. Griffith. "Inspiration," *Bibliotheca Sacra*, CXVIII, 469 (January, 1961), 41-45.

Vos, Johannes G. "Bible." In *The Encyclopedia of Christianity*, ed. Edwin H. Palmer, I, 654-662.

Warfield, Benjamin B. "Inspiration." In *International Standard Bible Encyclopaedia*, ed. James Orr, III, 1473-1483.

Witmer, John A. "The Biblical Evidence for the Verbal-Plenary Inspiration of the Bible," *Bibliotheca Sacra*, CXXI, 483 (July-September, 1964), 243-252.

B. Larger Works

Anderson, Stanley E. *Our Dependable Bible*. Grand Rapids: Baker Book House, 1960.

Boettner, Loraine. *Studies in Theology*. "The Inspiration of the Scriptures." Philadelphia: Presbyterian and Reformed Publishing Co. 1967.

Bowman, Allen. *Is the Bible True?* Westwood, New Jersey: Fleming H. Revell Company, 1965.

Can I Trust My Bible? (Anthology.)   Chicago: Moody Press, 1963.

DeHoff, George W. *Alleged Bible Contradictions Explained.* Grand Rapids: Baker Book House, 1950.

Engelder, T. E.   *Scripture Cannot Be Broken.* St. Louis: Concordia Publishing House, 1944.

Gaussen, L. *The Inspiration of the Holy Scriptures.* Chicago: Moody Press, 1949.   (Reprinted.)

Haley, John W. *Alleged Discrepancies of the Bible.* Andover: Warren F. Draper, 1874.   (Reprinted, Baker.)

Harris, R. Laird. *Inspiration and Canonicity of the Bible.* Grand Rapids: Zondervan Publishing House, 1957.

Henry, Carl F. H. ed. *Revelation and the Bible.* Grand Rapids: Baker Book House, 1958.

Lightner, Robert P. *The Saviour and the Scriptures.* Philadelphia: Presbyterian and Reformed Publishing Company, 1966.

Saphir, Adolph. *The Divine Unity of Scripture.* London: Hodder and Stoughton, 1892.

Stonehouse, Ned B., ed. *The Infallible Word.* Philadelphia: Presbyterian and Reformed Publishing Company, rev., 1968.

Walvoord, John F., ed. *Inspiration and Interpretation.* Grand Rapids: Wm. B. Eerdmans Publishing Company, 1957.

Warfield, Benjamin B. *The Inspiration and Authority of the Bible.* Philadelphia: Presbyterian and Reformed Publishing Company, 1948.

Wenger, J. C. *God's Word Written.* Scottdale, Pennsylvania: Herald Press, 1966.

Wight, Fred Hartley. *Our Inspired Bible.* Butler, Indiana: The Higley Press, 1960.

Young, Edward J. *Thy Word Is Truth.* Grand Rapids: Wm. B. Eerdmans Publishing Company, 1957.